Teaching Wright's
Native Son

Approaches to Teaching World Literature

Joseph Gibaldi, series editor

For a complete listing of titles,
see the last pages of this book.

Approaches to Teaching Wright's *Native Son*

Edited by

James A. Miller

The Modern Language Association of America
New York   1997

For information about obtaining permission to reprint material from
MLA book publications, send your request by mail (see address below),
e-mail (permissions@mla.org), or fax (212 533-0680).

Library of Congress Cataloging-in-Publication Data

Approaches to teaching Wright's Native son/
edited by James A. Miller
p. cm. — (Approaches to teaching world literature : 58)
Includes index.
ISBN 0-87352-739-9 (cloth). — ISBN 0-87352-740-2 (pbk.)
1. Wright, Richard, 1908–1960. Native son. 2. Wright, Richard,
1908–1960—Study and teaching. 3. Afro-Americans in literature—
Study and teaching. I. Miller, James A., 1944–   . II. Series.
PS3545.R815N325   1997
813'.52—dc21   96-40462
ISSN 1059-1133

Cover illustration for the paperback edition: still from the
1950 film version of *Native Son*, with Richard Wright shown
in the role of Bigger Thomas. Photograph: Kisch/Photofest.

Set in Caledonia and Bodoni. Printed on recycled paper

Published by The Modern Language Association of America
10 Astor Place, New York, New York 10003-6981

CONTENTS

Preface to the Series   vii

Preface to the Volume   ix

PART ONE: MATERIALS *James A. Miller*

Readings for Students   3

The Instructor's Library   3
   Reference Works   4
   Critical Studies   4
   Background Studies   6

PART TWO: APPROACHES

Introduction   11

Encountering the Text(s)

Native Son: Six Versions Seeking Interpretation   16
   Jerry W. Ward Jr.

Seeing *Native Son*   22
   Robert J. Butler

Teaching *Native Son* in a German Undergraduate
   Literature Class   28
   Klaus Schmidt
Literacy and the Liberation of Bigger Thomas   35
   Melba Joyce Boyd

Native Son and the Dynamics of the Classroom

Native Son as Project   42
   Philip Cohen and Doreen Fowler

Race and the Teaching of *Native Son*   48
   Garrett H. White

A Missionary to "Her People" Teaches *Native Son*   54
   Martha Satz

Native Son and Its Readers   67
   Robert Felgar

On Women, Teaching, and *Native Son*   75
   Farah Jasmine Griffin

Teaching Interculturalism: Symbiosis, Interpretation
    and *Native Son*   81
    James C. Hall

Specific Approaches

The Covert Psychoanalysis of *Native Son*   89
    Leonard Cassuto

Native Son as Depiction of a Carceral Society   95
    Virginia Whatley Smith

Lessons in Truth: Teaching Ourselves and
    Our Students *Native Son*   102
    SDiane A. Bogus

Max, Media, and Mimesis: Bigger's Representation
    in *Native Son*   112
    Michael Bérubé

Doing the (W)Right Thing: Approaching Wright and Lee   120
    Gary Storhoff

Contributors and Survey Participants   127

Works Cited   129

Index   139

PREFACE TO THE SERIES

In *The Art of Teaching* Gilbert Highet wrote, "Bad teaching wastes a great deal of effort, and spoils many lives which might have been full of energy and happiness." All too many teachers have failed in their work, Highet argued, simply "because they have not thought about it." We hope that the Approaches to Teaching World Literature series, sponsored by the Modern Language Association's Publications Committee, will not only improve the craft—as well as the art—of teaching but also encourage serious and continuing discussion of the aims and methods of teaching literature.

The principal objective of the series is to collect within each volume different points of view on teaching a specific literary work, a literary tradition, or a writer widely taught at the undergraduate level. The preparation of each volume begins with a wide-ranging survey of instructors, thus enabling us to include in the volume the philosophies and approaches, thoughts and methods of scores of experienced teachers. The result is a sourcebook of material, information, and ideas on teaching the subject of the volume to undergradates.

The series is intended to serve nonspecialists as well as specialists, inexperienced as well as experienced teachers, graduate students who wish to learn effective ways of teaching as well as senior professors who wish to compare their own approaches with the approaches of colleagues in other schools. Of course, no volume in the series can ever substitute for erudition, intelligence, creativity, and sensitivity in teaching. We hope merely that each book will point readers in useful directions; at most each will offer only a first step in the long journey to successful teaching.

Joseph Gibaldi
Series Editor

PREFACE TO THE VOLUME

Widely regarded as a central work in twentieth-century African American literature, Richard Wright's *Native Son* nevertheless occupies a somewhat tense and ambiguous position in the contemporary classroom. Although often invoked, Wright's masterpiece is taught less often than its canonical status would suggest—or, at least, this is what the responses from teachers surveyed in preparation for this volume indicate. One reason for not teaching *Native Son* is that it shocks, provokes, divides, and alienates readers, much as it did when it was first published in 1940. Another is that the impressive growth of African American literature and literary studies over the past several decades has tended to decenter fixed notions of an African American literary canon, and this decentering has affected how—and, indeed, whether—*Native Son* is taught in the classroom. For example, teachers today are much less inclined to approach *Native Son* as *the* representative work of African American fiction than they were in the 1970s. The old debate about whether *Native Son* should be regarded as a work of art or as a sociological document has been largely displaced by other questions, often shaped by the concerns of contemporary critical theory. Still, most teachers who teach *Native Son* acknowledge that it is virtually impossible to separate Wright's art from his politics or the power of his fiction from its roots in the apparently intractable problem of race in American society. The choice to teach *Native Son* automatically locates teachers and students in a highly charged social and artistic terrain that requires considerable skill to navigate.

Why do teachers teach *Native Son*? What assumptions do they make about the novel? What aspects of it do they emphasize and why? Is it possible to strike a balance between the literary and extraliterary values of the novel? Questions such as these informed the responses of the teachers surveyed for the volume, and they guided me as I sought to assemble a collection of essays that reflected not only the richness and complexity of Wright's novel but also the wide range of approaches to teaching it.

Answers to the questions in large measure dictated the content of this book. They indicate that *Native Son* is taught most often in surveys of African American literature but also in surveys of American literature, in introductory literature courses, and in specialized courses (The Modern Novel; African American Literature and the City). It is taught in introductory, advanced, and graduate courses; in prisons, private colleges, community colleges, and large private and public universities. Therefore we should not be surprised that the novel is taught from wide-ranging perspectives or that contributors bring different emphases to their teaching. Some contributors are concerned primarily with indicating how a particular critical or theoretical approach informs their teaching; others are concerned with particular pedagogical challenges created by the introduction of *Native Son* into the classroom. They all, however, are united in their fascination with the continuing vitality of *Native Son* and in their commitment to engaging their students in the complexities of a novel well worth studying.

Many people need to be thanked for their help in the preparation of this volume: the contributors, for their enthusiasm, their willingness to share their diverse approaches to *Native Son*, and especially their patience; Elaine Garrahy, assistant to the dean of faculty at Trinity College, Connecticut, for typing the manuscript; my student assistant, Elizabeth Duncan, for assisting in the preparation of the bibliography; the participants in my NEH Summer Seminars Four Classic African American Novels for their lively and stimulating conversations about the continuing relevance of Wright's work; Joseph Gibaldi, for caring about the project and helping me to bring it to a successful conclusion; and Edjohnetta, Ayisha, and John, for keeping my attention focused on the important issues.

James A. Miller
Trinity College, Connecticut

Part One

MATERIALS

Readings for Students

The amount of time most teachers allocate to *Native Son* leaves little room for secondary reading, and most respondents to the MLA survey of teachers of Richard Wright prefer that students encounter the novel on its own terms. As one respondent noted, "The novel alone is a struggle for many of them." With the exception of teachers of advanced literature courses or seminars devoted specifically to Wright, teachers of the novel recommend rather than require background or critical reading. Those concerned with locating *Native Son* in the broader context of Wright's work most often cite Wright's "The Ethics of Living Jim Crow," "Blueprint for Negro Writing," "How Bigger Was Born," "I Tried to Be a Communist," *Twelve Million Black Voices, American Hunger*, his introduction to St. Clair Drake and Horace Cayton's *Black Metropolis*, Michel Fabre's *The Unfinished Quest of Richard Wright*, and Margaret Walker's *Richard Wright: Daemonic Genius* (see also Fabre's review of this book). For judgments about Wright's place in African American literary tradition by his contemporaries, they recommend Ralph Ellison's "Richard Wright's Blues" and "Remembering Richard Wright" and James Baldwin's "Everybody's Protest Novel," "Many Thousands Gone," and "Alas, Poor Richard." They also recommend the following sources: Keneth Kinnamon's "*Native Son*: The Personal, Social, and Political Background"; George Kent's "Richard Wright: Blackness and the Adventure of Western Culture"; the Richard Wright issue of *Callaloo*; Harold Bloom's *Major Literary Characters: Bigger Thomas* and *Richard Wright*; Yoshinobu Hakutani's *Critical Essays on Richard Wright*; Joyce Ann Joyce's *Richard Wright's Art of Tragedy*; Kinnamon's *New Essays on Native Son*; and C. James Trotman's *Richard Wright: Myths and Realities*. For social and historical background, several instructors recommend John Hope Franklin's *From Slavery to Freedom* and Harold Cruse's *The Crisis of the Negro Intellectual*. Teachers also note students' need for background materials on naturalism and existentialism to understand the philosophical tensions of the novel.

The Instructor's Library

Scholarship on Richard Wright and *Native Son* has continued unabated since the resurrection of his literary reputation in the late 1960s. Although the following checklist of reference works and critical studies only samples the existing scholarship, it does contain the works that survey respondents most often identified as essential reading for teachers of *Native Son*. In addition to the checklist, instructors are encouraged to keep up with the *Richard Wright Newsletter*, the biannual publication of the Richard Wright Circle (Northeastern Univ., Dept. of English, 480 Nightingale Hall, Boston, MA 02115), and such journals as *African American Review* (formerly *Black American Literature Forum*), *Callaloo*, *CLA Journal*, and *MELUS*. Instructors should also consult the yearly bibliographies of the MLA and *American Literature*.

Reference Works

Charles T. Davis and Michel Fabre's *Richard Wright: A Primary Bibliography* offers a comprehensive listing of published and unpublished works by Wright. *A Richard Wright Bibliography: Fifty Years of Criticism and Commentary, 1933–1982*, compiled by Kinnamon with the assistance of Joseph Benson, Michel Fabre, and Craig Werner, is the most comprehensive and definitive bibliography on Wright through 1982. Having over thirteen thousand annotated items, it is an indispensable reference. In addition, many teachers cite John M. Reilly's *Richard Wright: The Critical Reception* as an extremely valuable reference, particularly for instructors concerned with locating *Native Son* in its historical context.

Critical Studies

Book-Length Studies

The most often cited biographical studies are Fabre's notable *Unfinished Quest* and *The World of Richard Wright*. Teachers also have high praise for Kinnamon's *The Emergence of Richard Wright: A Study in Literature and Society*. Some recommend Constance Webb's *Richard Wright: A Biography*, Addison Gayle Jr.'s *Richard Wright: Ordeal of a Native Son*, and Margaret Walker's *Richard Wright: Daemonic Genius*. Other biographies are Robert Felgar's *Richard Wright*, Russell Brignano's *Richard Wright: An Introduction to the Man and His Work*, Dan McCall's *The Example of Richard Wright*, David Bakish's *Richard Wright*, John A. Williams's *The Most Native of Sons*, and Robert Bone's *Richard Wright*.

Joyce's *Richard Wright's Art of Tragedy*, the most often cited critical reference for both students and teachers of *Native Son*, is highly recommended for its careful attention to the artistry of Wright's novel, as is Edward Margolies's *The Art of Richard Wright*. Eugene E. Miller's *Voice of a Native Son: The Poetics of Richard Wright* also focuses its attention on the aesthetic basis of Wright's achievement. Katherine Fishburn's *Richard Wright's Hero: The Faces of a Rebel-Victim* includes a detailed analysis of Bigger Thomas as both social rebel and victim, while Robert Butler's Native Son: *The Emergence of a New Black Hero* examines Bigger's possibilities for heroic action.

Important discussions of the political implications of *Native Son* appear in Donald B. Gibson's *The Politics of Literary Expression: A Study of Major Black Writers* and Richard Kostelanetz's *Politics in the African-American Novel.*

Collections of Essays

In addition to four journal issues devoted to Richard Wright (*Negro Digest* 18, 1968; *CLA Journal* 12, 1969; *Callaloo* 9, 1986; and *Mississippi Quarterly* 42, 1989), instructors cite the proceedings of the Third Annual Institute for Afro-American Culture at the University of Iowa, *Richard Wright and His Influence* (Ray and Farnsworth). Richard Abcarian's *Richard Wright's* Native Son: *A Critical Handbook*—unfortunately out of print—contains a selection of essays by Wright; an excellent sampling of contemporary reviews; Baldwin's "Many Thousands Gone"; Ellison's "The World and the Jug"; and essays by Cecil Brown, Eldridge Cleaver, and James Emmanuel, among others. The selection of essays on Wright in Donald B. Gibson's *Five Black Writers* includes Herbert Hill, Arna Bontemps, and Saunders Redding's "Reflections on Richard Wright: A Symposium on an Exiled Native Son" and essays by Maurice Charney, Nick Aaron Ford, and Redding. Houston A. Baker Jr.'s *Twentieth Century Interpretations of* Native Son: *A Collection of Critical Essays* reprints Wright's "How Bigger Was Born," contemporary opinion by Malcolm Cowley and Dorothy Canfield Fisher, Baldwin's "Many Thousands Gone," Nelson Algren's "Remembering Richard Wright," and essays by Baker, Robert Bone, Donald Gibson, Irving Howe, George Kent, and Dan McCall. Hakutani's *Critical Essays on Richard Wright* consists of nineteen essays, many of them reprints, but some of them new: by Nina Cobb, Gibson, Hakutani, Reilly, and Fred Standley, among others. Richard Macksey and Frank E. Moorer's *Richard Wright: A Collection of Critical Essays* includes important essays on *Native Son* by Gibson, Maria Mootry, Paul Siegal, and Kingsley Widmer. A compilation of essays first presented at the Richard Wright Literary Symposium in 1985 at West Chester University, Trotman's *Richard Wright: Myths and Realities* contains contemporary responses to the works of Wright, including essays by Joseph Bozziock, Elizabeth Ciner, Robert L. Douglas, Paul Newlin, Stephen Soitos, and Nagueyalti Warren. Bloom's *Major Literary Characters: Bigger, Richard Wright,* and *Richard Wright's* Native Son reprint representative extracts and critical essays on Wright and his work, including an excellent sampling of contemporary critical opinion. Teachers will find Bloom's *Richard Wright's* Native Son particularly useful; it contains ten interpretations published between 1969 and 1987, in addition to Joseph T. Skerrett Jr.'s "Composing Bigger: Wright and the Making of *Native Son*." *Major Literary Characters* reprints "How Bigger Was Born" and eleven essays that focus on the character of Bigger Thomas. The five essays in Kinnamon's *New Essays on* Native Son move beyond the old debate about art versus propaganda in *Native Son* to bring new theoretical and scholarly perspectives to bear on the novel. Henry Louis Gates Jr. and K. A. Appiah's *Richard Wright: Critical Perspectives Past and Present* contains a sampling of contemporary reviews of Wright's major work and twenty-two essays, including essays on *Native Son* by Baker, Barbara Foley, Barbara Johnson, Joyce, Kinnamon, Ross Pudaloff, and Laura E. Tanner.

Uncollected Essays

The best source for recent unpublished essays on Richard Wright and *Native Son* is *The Richard Wright Newsletter*. The first number of volume 1 includes a bibliography of works published between 1989 and 1991; the first number of volume 2 includes Kinnamon's supplement to *A Richard Wright Bibliography*.

Background Studies

The general history of African Americans that is mentioned most often by instructors is Franklin's *From Slavery to Freedom*. Other works recommended are John Blassingame's *The Slave Community* and August Meier and Elliott Rudwick's *From Plantation to Ghetto*. For studies of the historical bases of African American cultural traditions, instructors highly recommend Lawrence Levine's *Black Culture and Black Consciousness: Afro-American Folk Thought from Slavery to Freedom* and Eugene Genovese's *Roll, Jordan, Roll: The World the Slaves Made*. Some instructors point to John Dollard's *Caste and Class in a Southern Town* as a classic study of the conditions in the jim crow South that helped to mold Wright's consciousness. Dan T. Carter's *Scottsboro: A Tragedy of the American South* is also cited as an illuminating study of one of the most celebrated trials of the 1930s; the Scottsboro case anticipated the furor surrounding the Nixon case in Chicago, which Wright incorporated into *Native Son*. Drake and Cayton's *Black Metropolis* is highly recommended as a seminal study of Chicago's black community through World War II, as is Wright's photo-essay *Twelve Million Black Voices* and Spencer R. Crew's exhibition catalog, *Field to Factory: Afro-American Migration, 1915–1940*. James R. Grossman's *Land of Hope: Chicago, Black Southerners, and the Great Migration* is also recommended as a valuable historical study.

For further background on black life, respondents recommended W. E. B. Du Bois's *The Souls of Black Folk* and William Grier and Price Cobb's *Black Rage*.

Communism and Marxism

Cruse's *The Crisis of the Negro Intellectual* is most often cited as a key work for understanding Wright's relation to Marxism and the Communist Party; Mark Naison's *Communists in Harlem during the Depression* is cited almost as often. Another important study is Cedric Robinson's *Black Marxism: The Making of the Black Radical Tradition*. The documents compiled by Philip S. Foner and

Herbert Shapiro in *American Communism and Black Americans: A Documentary History, 1930–1934* offer fascinating insights into the policies of the Communist Party toward the black community during this period. Robin D. G. Kelley's *Hammer and Hoe: Alabama Communists during the Great Depression* offers a complex view of black, working-class radicalism in Alabama during the 1930s; Kelley's study goes a long way toward overturning the view, implicit in works like Wilson Record's *The Negro and the Communist Party*, that the black community was simply the passive receptacle of Communist ideology. Although Wright receives scant mention in the following works, they help illuminate the milieu of literary radicalism that nourished him: Daniel Aaron's *Writers on the Left: Episodes in American Literary Communism*, James Gilbert's *Writers and Partisans: A History of Literary Radicalism in America*, James F. Murphy's *The Proletarian Moment: The Controversy over Leftism in Literature*, and Walter B. Rideout's *The Radical Novel in the United States, 1900–1954*. Wright's "I Tried to Be a Communist"—published in Richard Crossman's *The God That Failed*—and *American Hunger* should ideally be read against this background.

The Literary Tradition

For discussions of Wright's relation to the African American literary tradition, instructors recommend Robert Stepto's *From behind the Veil: A Study of Afro-American Narrative* and "I Thought I Knew These People: Richard Wright and the Afro-American Literary Tradition," Valerie Smith's *Self-Discovery and Authority in Afro-American Narrative*, Gibson's *The Politics of Literary Expression*, Baker's *Blues, Ideology, and Afro-American Literature: A Vernacular Theory* and *Workings of the Spirit: The Poetics of Afro-American Women's Writing*, Gates's *The Signifying Monkey: A Theory of Afro-American Literary Criticism*, Michael G. Cooke's *Afro-American Literature in the Twentieth Century: The Achievement of Intimacy*, Melvin Dixon's *Ride Out the Wilderness: Geography and Identity in Afro-American Literature*, Gayle's *The Way of the New World: The Black Novel in America*, Bernard W. Bell's *The Afro-American Novel and Its Tradition*, and Robert Bone's *The Negro Novel in America*.

When Wright is mentioned in relation to American or European literary traditions, the writers most often invoked are Theodore Dreiser and Fyodor Dostoevsky. Essays exploring the connections between Wright and these writers include Hakutani's "*Native Son* and *American Tragedy*: Two Different Interpretations of Crime and Guilt" and "Richard Wright and American Naturalism," Tony Magistrale's "From St. Petersburg to Chicago: Wright's *Crime and Punishment*," and Kenneth T. Reed's "*Native Son*: An American *Crime and Punishment*." Teachers should also consult Michael F. Lynch's *Creative Revolt: A Study of Wright, Ellison, and Dostoevsky*. For Wright's relation to existentialism, teachers recommend Nathan A. Scott Jr.'s "The Dark and Haunted Tower of Richard Wright," Steven J. Rubin's "Richard Wright and Albert

Camus: The Literature of Revolt," and Kingsley Widmer's "Black Existentialism: Richard Wright." Carla Cappetti's *Writing Chicago: Modernism, Ethnography, and the Novel* locates Wright in a different context, with James T. Farrell and Nelson Algren in the tradition of urban writing exemplified by the Chicago school of sociology. Finally, Fabre's *Richard Wright: Books and Writers*, based on a study of Wright's library and archives, meticulously documents Wright's reading.

APPROACHES

Introduction

The revival of interest in Richard Wright's *Native Son* and its widespread introduction into American college and university classrooms coincided exactly with a particular moment in American life during the late 1960s, a period of pervasive student unrest on college campuses and of black militancy and black rebellion in many of America's cities. The significant increase in black student enrollments at predominantly white institutions in the aftermath of the assassination of Martin Luther King Jr. and the concurrent proliferation of demands for black studies programs brought into sharp relief the need for more serious academic attention to African American history and culture. In this context, Wright's achievement gained a new status, and Bigger Thomas, his most enduring fictional creation, reemerged, as Wright had hoped and predicted in "How Bigger Was Born," as a "symbolic figure of American life, a figure who would hold within him the prophecy of our future" (522). Bigger Thomas became a powerful signifier of the depths of black alienation and rage that seemed so palpable in the nation's cities.

More than half a century after its publication, *Native Son* continues to fascinate, repel, and divide its readers—fulfilling the grim vow Wright made after the enthusiastic critical reception of his first collection of short stories, *Uncle Tom's Children*: "I swore to myself that if I ever wrote another book, no one would ever weep over it; that it would be so hard and deep that they would have to face it without the consolation of tears" (*Native Son* 531). Wright, as St. Clair Drake and Horace Clayton note in their preface to *Black Metropolis*, took immense satisfaction in "wielding the verbal sledge-hammer and twisting the literary stiletto" (xli), and in *Native Son* Wright's choice of language, plot, and theme seems calculated to shock, to provoke, to outrage.

Bigger Thomas is poor, uneducated, and alienated from virtually everything in his environment; he is also a bully, hostile and menacing. By deliberately withholding the possibility of pity for Bigger—at least as he is initially presented—Wright undercuts the expectations of readers on both sides of the ideological spectrum, forcing readers to confront the violent emotions and behavior of a sullen black youth in 1930s Chicago.

Violence is indeed the hallmark of *Native Son*, the source of its relentless pace in books 1 and 2 and the basis of Bigger Thomas's development as a character. Two murders—one apparently accidental, the other deliberate; one of a young, wealthy, liberal white woman, the other of Bigger's poor, black girlfriend—trigger the breakneck pace of the first two books of the novel, plunging readers into the welter of racial stereotypes and sexual mythology that reinforce the racial status quo. The final book of the novel struggles to make sense of what Bigger has done. When Bigger announces, to Max's dismay and terror in the final scene of the novel, "What I killed for, I *am*! . . . What I killed for must have been good" (501), Bigger is arguing that violence is an act of self-creation and liberation for oppressed people—perhaps the only option available in a society that withholds or denies any sense of common humanity. At the same time, Wright's portrayal of Bigger's odyssey is skillfully linked to Wright's clinical dissection of another kind of violence—the immediate economic, political, and social forces that impinge on and shape Bigger's consciousness. Behind the concrete and oppressive reality of Bigger's environment, of course, stands the long and pervasive legacy of racism in the United States. Bigger Thomas therefore emerges as both a threat to the social order and an indictment of its structural failings.

Wright's radical politics, above all his membership in the American Communist Party at the time of the publication of *Native Son*, have always invited political readings of the novel, particularly of the third book, which continues to provoke debates among critics. The eloquent defense of Bigger by Bigger's attorney, Max, is regarded by some readers as a crude ideological intrusion of Wright's Marxist views into the fabric of the novel, a serious aesthetic flaw. Indeed, one of the critical controversies about *Native Son* revolves around the issue of how to interpret the final scene between Bigger and Max. The debate raises the larger, perennial question of the relation between politics and art: whether *Native Son* should be read primarily as a social and political statement or as a work of literature. Similarly, readers and critics tend to divide on the question of Bigger Thomas's character, his capacity for moral growth and insight, his accountability for his actions. Is Bigger a racial archetype or a racial stereotype? rebel or victim? hero or antihero? How does one reconcile Bigger's claims of human agency and free will with the grim, environmental determinism of *Native Son*? Who is responsible for the tragedy of Bigger Thomas?

Clearly, how teachers answer these questions will influence their approach to *Native Son*. The fifteen contributors to this volume propose significantly different answers—and raise other questions. Many factors determine how one teaches *Native Son*: the broad social and political climate; the institutional setting; the social, sexual, and racial composition of the class; and the teacher's social, sexual, and racial identity. Other factors are the nature and level of the course, the time alloted to the novel, and the teacher's judgment about which aspects of the novel are most important to teach. *Native Son* therefore occupies a central space in the complex and constantly shifting dynamics that define pedagogical practice. As the following essays demonstrate, it is the space where these dynamics often converge and sometimes collide.

The approaches explored in "Encountering the Text(s)" range from close textual analysis to consideration of the political and moral dimensions of the novel. The contributors differ, too, in their definitions of pedagogy, of what constitutes an approach to a text as highly charged as *Native Son*. What some teachers do in the classroom is shaped by the theoretical framework; what others do derives from a careful consideration of student response. These concerns sometimes overlap and sometimes do not.

Jerry W. Ward Jr. explores the possibilities of teaching *Native Son* by examining the various incarnations of the novel in two stage versions, two films, and the unexpurgated Library of America edition of the novel. By encouraging students to compare these texts, Ward argues, teachers not only heighten students' understanding of the politics of representation but also foreground the ways in which readers interact with texts, creating meaning in the process. Robert Butler describes his experiences teaching *Native Son* in three radically different places: an undergraduate seminar for seniors, a junior high school class, and an African American literature course at Attica Correctional Facility. Despite the differences he encountered among students in these settings, Butler found all of them fascinated by the power of the novel. Butler sees his challenge as a teacher "to prod the students to think beyond their interpretations" and to move them toward a more complicated reading of *Native Son*, one rooted in a deeper appreciation of Wright's artistic vision. Klaus Schmidt discusses the challenges of teaching *Native Son* to German undergraduates, challenges that seem remarkably similar to those faced by American teachers. Like Butler, Schmidt emphasizes a close critical reading of the novel, a reading that rejects an either-or approach to Wright's themes and characterization, seeking instead a greater appreciation of the textual complexity and artistry of *Native Son*. Whereas both Butler and Schmidt emphasize the primacy of the text, Melba Boyd insists on the continued political relevance of Wright's vision, emphasizing the parallels between the novel and contemporary American life. Bigger Thomas is alive and well in America's cities and in the American psyche, Boyd argues—as the Willie Horton episode of the 1988 presidential election campaign makes eminently clear. By pointing to those aspects of Wright's social and political critique that continue to resonate in American life, she demonstrates how "the teaching of *Native Son* involves a moral lesson for us all."

The essays in section 2 pay close attention to the problems of introducing this powerful and potentially polarizing novel into the classroom. Laura Quinn relates the various kinds of resistance she encounters when teaching *Native Son* to her students at a small, expensive private college in Pennsylvania. For Quinn, the best way to confront these acts of reader resistance is to mediate her students' experience of *Native Son* "by interactions with the historical complexities of its production and reception." By guiding her students through the various contexts in which *Native Son* has been read and received—historical, cultural, critical—Quinn challenges them to constantly reread and rethink their visceral responses to the novel and to sharpen their sense of African American literary history. Garrett H. White foregrounds the issue of race in his approach to the novel, suggesting ways in which "we can confront and employ race in our teaching very profitably." Invoking W. E. B. Du Bois's paradigm of double consciousness, White describes a model for the kind of rhetorical dexterity he believes is necessary if teachers and students are to avoid a false sense of security about the validity of their perspectives toward Bigger Thomas. Martha Satz argues that "reading texts, most especially reading texts by black authors in our culture, acutely involves one's racial positioning within the society." Against this backdrop, she explores her experiences teaching *Native Son* at a private university in Texas. We have not been schooled to discuss race, Satz observes, and her essay describes her systematic approach to creating a sophisticated, multilayered context that makes the teaching of *Native Son* possible and meaningful within the framework of a sustained discussion about race and culture. Robert Felgar describes how he combines reader-response criticism and cultural critique in an attempt to transform his classroom "from a morgue into a site of lively and productive debate and discussion." While acknowledging that different students will experience *Native Son* differently, he also argues that students can analyze and deal with some categories of responses. His essay discusses how he challenges "generic" readers—white men, black men, women—to move from their personal reactions to the novel to a more critically informed understanding of how their situations as readers influence their interpretation of *Native Son*. Farah Jasmine Griffin focuses on Wright's portrayal of women in *Native Son*, describing her students' anger and discomfort—and her own—in the face of an issue that concerns many contemporary readers and critics. Griffin carefully describes her strategies for "balancing a critique of Wright's treatment of women with an appreciation for the issues . . . that make the text of continuing relevance" to both students and teachers. Teachers must acknowledge Wright's sexism early in any discussion of *Native Son*, Griffin argues, while guiding students toward a more complex appreciation of Wright's powerful rendering of Bigger Thomas's urban environment. James Hall discusses ways of challenging the tendency among many students to "claim aesthetic, political, and cultural distance" from *Native Son*, a tendency that often results in the impulse "to rely on a few black students to provide both exegesis and testimony." Arguing that the challenge of teaching is to create a constructive interpretive community in the classroom, Hall emphasizes the transgressive nature of border crossings as a metaphor for the classroom. By interrogating the borders and boundaries in *Native Son*, he demonstrates how Wright asserts "the value of rational discourse, effective interpretation, and 'appropriate' cross-cultural investigation."

The essays in section 3 explore the teaching of *Native Son* in different contexts and from a variety of critical and theoretical perspectives. Leonard Cassuto relates the experience of teaching the novel in an interdisciplinary seminar on literary Darwinism. By focusing class discussion on Bigger Thomas as an individual rather than as an archetype, Cassuto hopes to overcome the distance that often separates the character from many readers. More important, Cassuto hopes to lead his students to a basic understanding of key terms in psychoanalytic thought, thus linking a psychoanalytic reading with the powerful social themes of *Native Son*. Virginia Whatley Smith applies to *Native Son* the theoretical framework of Michel Foucault's *Discipline and Punish*, demonstrating how Foucault's theories underscore the depth of Wright's critique of a carceral society. SDiane Bogus is concerned with the moral values—or lack of them—expressed in *Native Son.* Her approach to the novel hinges on convincing her readers and students to overturn established critical opinion and see the novel in a new light. She raises searching questions about the ethical and moral vision of *Native Son* and about the moral obligations of teachers of the novel. The remaining two essays examine various relations between *Native Son* and the mass media. Michael Bérubé focuses on the problem of "African American representation in the legal and in the mimetic sense" in *Native Son,* beginning with a careful analysis of the legal arguments that seek to define and represent Bigger Thomas. *Native Son,* Bérubé says, "is less concerned with Bigger's representativeness than with Bigger's multiple representations and what these might tell us about the processes by which blackness is constructed and consumed." Gary Storhoff's essay is a fitting one to conclude this volume, for it suggests the ways in which *Native Son* still resonates with the experiences of contemporary American students. Storhoff's essay also testifies to the continuing power of the mass media to shape our lives. By teaching his students how Wright's novel anticipates Spike Lee's themes in *Do the Right Thing,* Storhoff expands the context of both *Native Son* and Lee's film, challenging his students to develop "a greater political, social, and moral alertness about the world before our eyes."

NOTE

This volume's quotations from *Native Son* are taken from the HarperPerennial 1993 edition, which restored the author's original text; Wright had made revisions (expurgations) in 1939 so that the work could be sold to the Book-of-the-Month Club. This volume's few quotations from the unrestored *Native Son* are taken from the HarperPerennial 1966 edition and indicated by a bracketed "1966" with the page number.

Native Son: Six Versions Seeking Interpretation

Jerry W. Ward Jr.

Few scholars would argue that Richard Wright's *Native Son* is not a classic in the histories of African American and American literature and criticism. Teachers assume that the novel's canonical status is secure, that well into the twenty-first century people will continue to read (or be told they ought to read) *Native Son*. There is, however, the danger that being a literary classic may resemble sainthood. Once canonized and iconized by the clergy, the saint may lose appeal among the laity and get lost in the liturgical archives, the Roman Catholic equivalent of literary criticism's wilderness. Fortunately, the fate of a novel is linked not to the production of miracles but to its power among readers as Burkean "equipment for living," that is, as a necessary aesthetic object and as an instrument for probing social constructions. That *Native Son* is still either invoked or evoked during major instances of urban rebellion in the United States attests to its extraliterary, prophetic power, or perhaps to our willingness to use the title *Native Son* as a marker of cultural literacy and as a metonym for Bigger Thomas. Whatever the case, anyone who teaches *Native Son* must be prepared to deal with the various ways in which the novel's main character may be concretized. In addition to the possibilities offered by the 1940 text, there are others that derive from two dramatized versions of the book (Paul Green's 1941 dramatization, with Wright, of *Native Son* and Green's 1968 revision of that play), two film transformations (1950 and 1986), and the unexpurgated Library of America edition of the novel (1991). For neither as teachers nor as readers are we free to stand outside engagements with the novel that have become increasingly hypertextual.

Critical interpretations of *Native Son* have tended to divide fairly neatly between "improper" readings of Wright's masterpiece as a social and political statement or a sociological document and "proper" readings of it as a powerful work of literature. "Improper" readings of *Native Son* still encourage the belief that "Bigger Thomas" is more than two words in a book that five decades ago significantly altered the tradition of American fiction. Perhaps "Bigger Thomas" is an odd stereotype, naming a conception or marking a loose description of certain dispossessed, disinherited, and dejected males in a dislocated United States. One sometimes has the vague feeling that "Bigger Thomas" is a mascon sign for an agonizing truth that attracts literarily because it enables one to criticize the signifier while maintaining a safe distance from its living referent.

A "proper," or traditional, reading of the novel (within a formalist paradigm) precludes the sociological heresy altogether and enables us, through our attention to the language of the text, to realize the timelessness of *Native Son*: the novel, instead of being the end of Wright's intentional creative process, is the origin of the reader's always re-creative process. In this context, it is worth pursuing the ways that succeeding generations of readers have constituted themselves around Wright's text and the ways that readers use language and experience to create meaning. In classroom discussions of *Native Son*, we teachers may find that differing weights given to meaning and significance in interpretation (Hirsch 209–44), particularly of the character of Bigger Thomas, lead to interpretive dead ends. One way of minimizing if not resolving the dilemma is to admit that our experiences as readers (or spectators) necessitate negotiation before we can reach provisional agreement about what is represented in a text, a dramatized text, or a film. If for example we are teaching the 1940 or 1993 text of *Native Son*, we can cast some light on the sources of the critical debates by including discussion of the stage versions of *Native Son* or the film versions. These versions (as specialized readings of the text) may help us expose how proper and improper readings are ultimately complementary, providing links between language and experience.

Keneth Kinnamon's introductory remarks for *New Essays on* Native Son and Arnold Rampersad's textual notes for the Library of America edition of the novel remind us that a book we may have in hand rarely matches the author's intentions. Having made a preliminary examination of letters, notes, typescripts, and galley and page proofs associated with the making of the first edition of *Native Son*, Kinnamon itemizes the major differences between Wright's original story and the 1940 text with which most readers are familiar. The author's changes have to do with style, improved opening and closing episodes, and the representation of sexuality. Wright seems to have taken more care to render dialect than in some of his earlier writing and to ensure that the vocabulary is intelligible to a general readership. Abandoning the original opening that focused on Bigger's disgust with religion, he replaced it with the rat scene that effectively illustrates the Thomas family's quality of life, shows Bigger's incipient violence, and foreshadows Bigger's fate (Kinnamon, *New Essays* 9). Some explicit sexual descriptions were deleted, and a poetic ending that exploited "the metaphorical dimension of fire in the original conclusion of *Native Son*" (10) was replaced by the simpler scene of Bigger's stoic accommodation to fate. The cumulative effect of some deletions regarding racial politics in book 3, Kinnamon suggests, is to tone down somewhat "the political message" and "also mitigate the artistic tedium their inclusion would increase" (15).

Potentially explosive aspects of the story, de-emphasized in the transition from manuscript to printed novel, may be amplified in the plays and films based on the 1940 text. The repressed elements (now available in the 1993 edition) erupt in the plays and films, increasing the stakes as we recognize that each new portrayal (reading, interpretation) relocates the images and ideas we associate with the words "Bigger Thomas."

Paul Green's dramatizations of *Native Son* in 1941 and 1968 are problematic examples of that transformation. Green suggests what his intentions were in a 1969 letter to William Brasmer. Regarding the 1941 version, Green wrote:

> I read the novel and finally decided I would tackle it. I made three stipulations—one being that I would have freedom to invent new characters and make editorial story changes where necessary, another being that I could make the Communist slant in the book comic when I felt like it, and last, that Richard Wright come and be with me during my dramatizing work—this last being necessary I felt for discussion purposes as I went along. . . . [Wright] didn't write any of the dramatization but he was of great help in that I could check matters with him.   (Brasmer 71)

The only new character invented is Miss Emmet, the white social worker. Her appearance at the moment the rat is being killed, as well as her name (*emmet* is a dialect word for "ant"), stresses how the Thomas family must contend with animal and human intrusions. But the reinvention of Bigger's girlfriend Bessie Mears as Clara Mears indicates that Green had access to a typescript of the novel. In the movie-theater episode deleted in the 1940 edition, Bigger's pal Jack refers to his girlfriend Clara (33).

Green did not exactly render the Communist slant comic, but the force of Marxist critique is softened. It has been claimed that the dramatization also softens Bigger's character, but the representation of Bigger in dialogue and action devoid of a narrator's control may actually intensify our ambivalence. The character may seem, as Ouida Campbell reported, "one half Mr. Green's Bigger—sensitive, misguided, puzzled about life in general; and the other half Wright's Bigger—full of hate and fear, cunning, but at the same time looking for an answer to the questions raised in his mind" (23).

As one moves between the 1941 play and the 1940 novel, it becomes apparent that Green did protest Bigger's innocence more than Wright. Green sought to minimize Bigger's responsibility for certain actions. Mary's seduction of Bigger is made quite noticeable. In the novel, she is virtually inarticulate as Bigger helps her to her room; in the play, she rambles on about politics, race, Bigger's hair, feelings—the novel's silence is replaced with sexually charged discourse (scene 4). This change makes us more aware of Mary's complicity (at economic, racial, class, and sexual levels) and Bigger's victimization. Bigger dramatized is less guilty. Green's character does not have the cold-bloodedness of Wright's Bigger. He does not kill Clara (Bessie); she is killed by a policeman's bullet (scene 8). These changes simplify matters and reduce Bigger's human dimensions. The swift movement of the dramatization does not allow us to probe much for complexity of character.

The shape of *Native Son* on stage radically diminishes the pleasure one discovers in working through the complexity of the novel. The use of ten scenes to represent the sequence of fear (scenes 1–4), flight (scenes 5–8), and fate (scenes 9 and 10) could be trivialized or read melodramatically as Bigger at Home, Bigger in the Streets, Bigger Meets the Daltons, Bigger in Mary's Bedroom, Bigger versus Britten, Bigger and Clara, Bigger Found Out by the Newspaperman, Bigger's Capture, Bigger's Trial, Bigger's Last Visitors. Such loose plotting may be a theatrical virtue, but it lessens the reader's or spectator's obligation to consider the serious waste of human resources in America. The spectacular receives priority.

Although in Green's 1968 revision of his and Wright's 1941 adaptation, none of the inserted references—to Chinese Communists, black power, and the Black Muslims—is sufficient to fit *Native Son* into the context of the 1960s, the revision does provide several changes that must not be overlooked. First, Green makes Buckley's argument and call for "imposing the penalty of death upon this miserable human being, Bigger Thomas" (76) the prologue. Since Buckley's call for the death penalty has been given a privileged position, Green reverses the ending of speeches at the trial (cf. Green 172–73 with Green and Wright 427–28). The lawyer, Max, now gets the last word. He also gets the last word in the final scene: the priest's voice intoning "I am the resurrection and the life" and the death chant of the prisoners in the 1941 version have been deleted. Although Green fails to update *Native Son*, his two dramatizations alert us to the importance of the drastic changes in the film versions of Wright's novel.

The 1950 film *Native Son*, in which Wright himself plays the role of Bigger Thomas, is a rather free interpretation of the book. It opens as a documentary on black Chicago, initiating one set of expectations. The voice-over—"Here is Hannah. Here is Vera. Here is Buddy. Here is Bigger"—echoes a first-grade reader of the 1940s. The film ends with the voice of Mr. Max:

> I left Bigger feeling that everything, including justice, was still unsettled. And today, I feel even less certain about innocence and guilt, crime and punishment, of the nature of man.

Within the frame created by these voices, the film alters *Native Son* in remarkable ways.

It is exceedingly difficult to talk about film without visual evidence, so I only draw attention to several features that lead to questions about eruptions and digressions from the printed text:

> Bessie is not a domestic worker but a waitress on the verge of having a career as a nightclub singer at Ernie's; Ernie's is not a "kitchen shack" but a rather elaborate nightspot that features a boxing exhibition, a band, and "the king of bebop" (a parody of Dizzy Gillespie?).
>
> Bigger is not twenty but twenty-five. Thus attention is shifted from the plight of the late adolescent to the adolescent behavior of adults.
>
> Immediately after he is employed by the Daltons, Bigger takes the car on a trial drive, which turns into a romantic interlude with Bessie. He drives the car into the Chicago slums to make a display of new status, takes Bessie to the Riverside Amusement Park and then to Lake Michigan for a swim.
>
> The nightmare sequence, which is part of Bigger's confession about killing Bessie, opens a psychological dimension that may reveal more about Wright than about Bigger Thomas. As Bigger kneels in a pile of coal with a bundle in hand, Bessie's ghost directs him to hide it in a field of whiteness. Bigger finds himself in a cotton field that reminds him of the farm where he grew up and of his lynched father, to whom he runs and cries. The father, however, is Britten (visually stereotyped as the overweight, cigar-smoking southern sheriff), who has discovered the bundle (Mary's head) and laughs grotesquely at Bigger.

Changes of this kind, and so telling a visual clue as the uncanny resemblance of Hannah and Miss Emmet to photographs of Wright's mother and grandmother, respectively, suggest that the 1950 film should be studied as an autobiographical meeting of character and creator or as a cinematic gloss on the unsaid in Wright's "How 'Bigger' Was Born." The film tips viewers over into the realm of the surreal. In contrast, the 1986 film developed from Richard Wesley's screenplay seems a very faithful translation of the 1940 novel.

At least one aspect of the 1986 film suggests how versions must be read against one another so that we can understand the motives behind our interpretations. In book 2 of the 1940 and 1991 editions of the novel, Bigger murders Bessie, and we cannot minimize the successive changes of her murder in other versions. In the dramatizations for the stage, she is killed by a policeman's bullet. In the 1950 film, she is glamorized and killed. In the 1986 film, all mention of her murder is erased; she simply vanishes. Seeing what happens to Bessie in various interpretations, we begin to appreciate more strongly how making sense of *Native Son* and of Bigger Thomas is wedded to medium and the politics of representation. If there is a stretching of artistic liberty in Green's getting Bigger Thomas off the hook in the matter of Bessie's death and if there is a certain political correctness in Green's not portraying, in 1986, the willful murder of a black woman by a black man, do such liberty and such correctness in (re)presentation now disavow Wright's intentions and throw *Native Son* into a writhing nest of race and gender?

What ultimately is the value of teaching *Native Son* by encouraging students to discover the links and disjunctures among the 1940 and 1991 editions of the novel and other versions? This approach promotes greater honesty in the study of literature, especially in the study of classic American texts, and foregrounds what older models of reading often repressed: that readers interact with texts, make meaning from signifiers and signifieds, and create their versions of the text (McCormick, Waller, and Flower 6). This approach provides an opportunity to test much that is currently argued in literary and cultural theory about information technologies and to expand the critical imagination while at the same time imposing on readers the responsibility to be accurate and thorough in understanding their role in literature as an event. Reading the film *Native Son* exposes in a new key why we continue to study literature and what "Bigger Thomas" can signify at different times. This process also increases readers' admiration of the artistic integrity of Richard Wright.

Seeing *Native Son*

Robert J. Butler

> The difficulty most critics have who wrote about *Native Son* is that they do not see Bigger Thomas. They see him with their outer eyes but not their inner eyes.
> —Donald B. Gibson

Over the years most readers of Richard Wright's *Native Son* have readily acknowledged its extraordinary power. One of the first reviewers of the novel remarked that it packed "a tremendous punch, something like a big fist through the windows of our complacent lives" (Hansen 47). More recently, Clarence Major described his first reading of the novel as "an overwhelming experience" (220), and John A. Williams observed, "What I remember most when I first read *Native Son* at age 14 or 15 was its relentless power" (1).

This power no doubt explains why Wright's novel teaches so well to such a wide range of students and in such a wide variety of courses. *Native Son* continues to wake up even the sleepiest bunch of students required to take freshman English, just as it shocks into attention the most sophisticated English majors in a senior seminar. In all my thirty years of teaching, I have never had a disappointing teaching experience with the novel—a claim I can make for no other book I regularly teach.

But if the novel's power is an important pedagogical asset, it can also present a formidable pedagogical challenge. Students often are so taken by the novel's force that they miss its subtleties and nuances, the complexities that make Wright's masterpiece so rich and perennially interesting. For this reason, I always allow a substantial amount of time for the novel in whatever course it appears, so that the students and I can read the text closely and discuss divergent interpretations carefully.

I recently taught *Native Son* in three very different courses: a senior seminar in modern literature taught to English majors at Canisius College, a survey course entitled The Hero in American Literature taught to Buffalo-area high school juniors, and an African American literature course taught to students in the college program at Attica Correctional Facility. The modern literature course put *Native Son* in a sequence that included Ibsen's *A Doll House*, Gogol's "The Overcoat," Zola's *La bête humaine*, Dostoevsky's *Notes from the Underground*, Silone's *Bread and Wine*, and Ionesco's *Rhinoceros*. The Hero in American Literature put *Native Son* in a syllabus that contained Crevecoeur's "What Is an American?," Thoreau's *Walden*, Whitman's "Song of Myself," Douglass's *Narrative*, James's *Daisy Miller*, Cather's *My Antonia*, Steinbeck's *The Grapes of Wrath*, and Theroux's *The Mosquito Coast*. The course in African American Literature placed *Native Son* in a third context of readings that included worksongs, spirituals, blues, Douglass's *Narrative*,

Locke's "The New Negro," Hughes's *The Weary Blues*, Hurston's *Their Eyes Were Watching God*, Ellison's *Invisible Man*, Walker's *The Color Purple*, and Naylor's *The Women of Brewster Place*. The composition of the classes in these three courses presented an even more diverse picture. The modern literature course at Canisius was taught to a coeducational group consisting mainly of white, middle-class students who ranged in age from twenty-one to twenty-three. The American literature course was taught to a coeducational group of seventeen-year-old white students who came mostly from suburban backgrounds. And the class at Attica was completely male, predominantly black and Hispanic, and ranged in age from people in their early twenties to those in their early fifties. Many of the Attica students came from social and economic backgrounds that bore a striking resemblance to Bigger Thomas's environment.

Despite these differences, all three classes quickly became fascinated by the power of *Native Son*. They read the novel enthusiastically and engaged in spirited and fruitful discussions about it and the issues it raises. The book forcefully opened eyes and awakened voices in each class, although each class saw and expressed very different things. The modern literature students were inclined to view Bigger as a quintessentially modern antihero who, like Dostoevsky's underground man, is overwhelmed by a social context that denies him a human identity and who, like Zola's Jacques Lantier, is destroyed by meaningless violence. My students at Attica offered a reading of *Native Son* that was a striking reverse of this, seeing Bigger as a revolutionary hero who, like Douglass, uses violence to gain his freedom from a racist society intent on reducing him to the level of an animal. The high school students tended to view Bigger in terms of the historical setting in which he is placed, partly because in the previous academic year they had taken courses in American history and a survey of American literature that is required by the New York State Board of Regents. Given the context of the Great Depression, they saw Bigger in naturalistic terms, as a victim of economic and social forces, an inversion of the rags-to-riches myth described in Alger's *Ragged Dick* and of the conversion myth described in Crevecoeur's "What Is an American?"

Teaching all three classes was a rewarding and exciting experience, since each group was deeply touched by the novel, thought carefully about it, and wanted to talk about it in a vigorous, honest, and open way. (Such strong reactions to a novel are certainly refreshing for a teacher who all too often these days is disappointed by student apathy.) Each group presented a truth about the novel that forced me to reexamine my own reading of the book. But in each class my task as a teacher was to prod the students to think beyond interpretations that usually derived from a first reading rooted in a sense of the novel's power. Just as Donald Gibson years ago did a great service to the scholarly community by reminding us that most readers of *Native Son* see only a small part of its complex vision, I wanted to enlarge my students' understanding of the novel, moving from what they saw when they first read it to a much more complicated approach to the book, an approach that would give them a fuller appreciation of Wright's vision. Keep in mind, however, that I didn't want them to lose their sense of the novel's power. If I had to choose between students' sensing a novel's power and their understanding its complexities, I would choose the former. But I did not want to make such a choice with *Native Son*, feeling that one's experience of the force of Wright's book is in fact increased when one becomes more aware of its richly nuanced vision, a vision that is as relevant to us today as it was to readers in 1940.

But how to get students from all three of my classes to experience these complexities without diminishing in any way for them the novel's emotional force? I began this process by discussing the novel's intricate narrative structure, which I am convinced is a key to the novel's complex themes. I reminded the students that Wright's "How Bigger Was Born" is still one of the most revealing commentaries on *Native Son*. In that essay Wright stresses that his writing of the novel was a difficult process taking many years and involving a number of artistic decisions. This revelation often comes as a shock to students, who see the novel as so "real" that they mistakenly conclude that it was sliced from Wright's own life and that all Wright had to do was directly transcribe his raw experiences. Students are productively surprised, therefore, when Wright tells them in his essay that he tried to write the opening scene twenty or thirty times, looking for a scene that was so carefully crafted that it would provide "the type of concrete event that would convey the motif of the entire scheme of the book, that would sound, in varied form, the note that was to be resounded throughout its length" (534).

I spent one whole class, therefore, analyzing and discussing the novel's opening scene, getting the students to see how it telescopes the entire novel by introducing themes, images, and symbols that resonate in most of the major episodes that follow. Then I showed them how the rest of the novel is as consciously designed as the opening scene, that it breaks into three main narrative segments, or books, each book divided into three major scenes. The students and I arrived at this rough skeletal outline of the novel:

Book 1

1. Bigger's killing of the rat
2. Bigger's near killing of Gus
3. Bigger's accidental killing of Mary

Book 2

1. Bigger's murder of Bessie
2. Bigger's escape from the authorities
3. Bigger's capture by the police

Book 3

1. Bigger's conversations in his cell

2. Bigger's dialogue with Max in the visiting room
3. Bigger's final talk with Max

With this outline I illustrated Wright's complex use of narrative structure. Rather than mechanically repeat scenes to make the same point about his central character, Wright uses repetition as a musical composer does to establish a theme at the beginning of a piece and then develop a set of variations on that theme, thereby enriching the music. Scenes in *Native Son* reverberate against one another to produce effects that become more complex as the novel develops. The initial scene, depicting Bigger as similar to the trapped animal he is forced to kill, centers the novel, and all the major scenes radiate from this center. But increasingly rich meanings are produced as Bigger grows, as experiences broaden his perspective and deepen his consciousness. The scenes progress, and Bigger becomes much more than a trapped animal—he indeed becomes "bigger" than all the stereotyped roles his environment imposes on him. Although he begins the novel as a naturalistic victim, he eventually attains no small measure of freedom and selfhood by existentially developing his consciousness and using that consciousness as a basis for human action.

Another way I tried to make the students aware of Bigger's human development was by having them study systems of images that Wright employs throughout these scenes, especially ocular images. In the first scene, for example, Bigger rubs his eyes to adjust his vision from total darkness to blinding light (1). Because the ensuing action takes place quickly and Bigger can see it only in a blur, he is forced to act in an unthinking, reflexive way. Bigger's vision is likewise defective in the poolroom scene, where he views Gus murderously through "the hard glint of his bloodshot eyes" (42), and also in Mary's pitch-black bedroom, where he accidentally kills her because he can neither physically see her nor mentally envision his situation. Ocular images are used for very different effect in books 2 and 3, which show Bigger becoming increasingly more able to see himself and his world, so that eventually he frees himself of the environmental determinants that blinded and trapped him in book 1. He clearly sees Bessie when he deliberately murders her, turning on the light to get a good view of her face. When he escapes from the authorities, he gradually develops a lucid vision of how he and other black people are treated in American society. Having a clear view of the world around him for the first time in his life, he can begin to gain emotional distance from and psychological control over that world. In this way, he takes crucial steps toward selfhood, planting seeds that eventually flower in book 3. At the end of the novel he no longer wants to "whirl and blot [people] from sight" (341) as he had wished earlier in book 3, but instead he desires to see them and himself as human beings. He comes to see Jan as someone who "had performed an operation upon his eyes" (333–34), and later he looks "straight into Max's eyes" when the two engage in conversation (402). As a result, Bigger is able to dismantle the psychological walls that previously obscured his vision and separated him not only from other people but also from his own human nature. The three major scenes of book 3, which show Bigger outwardly immobilized in jail but inwardly moving toward increased consciousness and a new sense of self, contrast sharply with the three major scenes of book 1, which portray Bigger as physically active but visually stunned and psychologically paralyzed. By the end of the novel he might still be invisible, like Ellison's invisible man, to those who lack his inward resources, but he is no longer blind to himself or to his world.

All the interrelated patterns of imagery in *Native Son* are designed to make us see Bigger's human development. Such imagery keeps reminding us that there are indeed "two Biggers" (292), the brutalized outward self that students have no trouble seeing and the "personal and private" self (526) that Wright asks them to see and that I hope they did see on the second and third readings I encouraged them to undertake. The furnace in which Bigger incinerates Mary's body is a good illustration. Although most students reacted in simple revulsion to this image, I tried to show them how Wright converts it into a symbol of Bigger's enflamed conscience. As Bigger continues to be troubled by this image, compulsively recalling it, it comes to reflect his guilt over killing another human being rather than his simple fear of being caught and punished by the authorities. In a similar way, his repeated imagining of Mary's severed head is anything but a reflection of satisfaction at having killed a white girl; on the contrary, it becomes a powerful sign of his moral revulsion from such violence. When Bigger dreams of running away and carrying Mary's head in a paper package, he discovers to his horror (and our surprise) that her head has turned into "his *own* head" (189). However much his outward self formed by society wants to relish violence, his inward self condemns such violence, seeing it as wrong and self-destructive.

By growing more aware of the highly conscious art of *Native Son*, my students came to appreciate what Wright meant when he said, "Bigger, as I saw and felt him, was a snarl of many realities; he had in him many levels of life" (526). It is my task as a teacher to help students see Bigger as Wright saw him, not as Buckley sees him, a monster (480), or as Max sees him, a boy (454) and a problem (455). Wright's art reveals itself only to close readers who are willing to discuss their views with other readers in a dialectic that is both aggressive and sensitive. It is only by sharing our partial views of *Native Son* that we do as readers what Bigger does as a character—we open our eyes to the complexity before us, seeing powerful details in a richly textured context. When we read at the beginning of book 2 that Bigger thinks he has "created a new life for himself" by killing Mary Dalton (119), we should not conclude that Wright meant him to be either a psychopath or a bold revolutionary. The scene is placed in a context of other scenes that enrich its meanings with qualifying ironies and paradoxes. Although violence has jarred Bigger out of a numbing paralysis that threatened to destroy him, it does not provide him with a full human identity. (Indeed, violence is nothing new for Bigger, and the killing of Mary Dalton only completes his mother's prophecy made early in the book, that he is heading for the gallows.) In the same way, when students read Bigger's claims at the end of the novel, "But what I killed for, I *am!*" and "What I killed for must've been good!" (501), they must pay attention to all the words in these two sentences, especially the word *for*. Although the Bigger of the opening scene is inclined to romanticize violence, little realizing how violence is a daily threat to him, the Bigger of the closing scene values not violence but those things that he became violent *for*: the personal freedom and autonomy he needs in order to construct a human self that can see and touch others not in violence but in love.

Luckily, none of my classes ever came up with a final or definitive interpretation that killed the text by arresting the text's possibilities for meaning. We arrived at many different interpretations of Wright's masterwork, depending on our various backgrounds and the contexts of readings in which we placed the novel. But in each class my purpose remained the same—to make students conscious of Wright's considerable art, an art that washes our minds free of labels and startles us into an awareness of new meanings. *Native Son* therefore is just as exciting a book for me to teach now as it was thirty years ago, when my students first opened my eyes to its power and I began to want to return the favor to them by introducing them to its artful complexities.

Teaching *Native Son* in a German Undergraduate Literature Class

Klaus Schmidt

In response to Henry Louis Gates Jr.'s call for close readings of African American literature that foregrounds "the most repressed element of Afro-American criticism: the language of the text" (*Figures* xviii), this essay focuses on the difficulty of conveying the textual complexity and artistry of a (black) American classic in the undergraduate classroom. *Native Son* has long been simplistically interpreted as no more than a social protest novel. The theme of marginality has been especially abused and oversimplified by black-and-white, either-or approaches to *Native Son*, and yet the theme is a focal point from which the complexity of the novel can be revealed. Uncorrected excerpts from papers presented in an undergraduate seminar that I taught at the University of Mainz, Germersheim—Richard Wright's *Native Son*: A Classic of (Black) American Literature—exemplify the problems German students have in understanding African American texts. Those problems are due mostly to the students' lack of experience with black literature and their lack of knowledge about black American culture and about literary theory. Unless we sharpen our students' sensitivity and emphasize the complexity and ambivalent character of black literary texts, works such as *Native Son* will continue to be discussed and taught simplistically instead of receiving the critical attention they deserve. The importance of the theme of marginality in *Native Son* is acknowledged both by authorities on Richard Wright and by students. Neglected, however, is the complex framework that determines the theme's narrative representation in the novel.

The complexity of marginality in *Native Son* has four principal aspects: (1) the protagonist's double consciousness and Janus-like position as both subject and object, (2) the mirror function of women's marginalization, (3) the male outsider's process of articulation encoded by an intricate blues syntax, and (4) the deictic relativity of inside and outside.

W. E. B. Du Bois's concept of double consciousness in the novel is expressed even in Wright's introduction, "How 'Bigger' Was Born":

> What made Bigger's social consciousness most complex was the fact that he was hovering unwanted between two worlds—between powerful America and his own stunted place in life—and I took upon myself the task of trying to make the reader feel this No Man's Land.　(527)

Bigger Thomas functions both as a product of the dominant discourse and as an autonomous individual. His ambivalent ontological status influences the text from the beginning. After the often-quoted rat scene in "Fear," Bigger serves as a personification of the black family's failure in an environment dominated by intolerable social conditions: "'Bigger, sometimes I wonder why I birthed you,' she [his mother] said bitterly" (6). Replying as a speaking subject, Bigger comments on himself as an addressed object: "Maybe you oughtn't've. Maybe you ought to left me where I was" (6). His objectification in the microcosm "black family" stands metonymically for his marginalization in the macrocosm "black community," which talks mostly about rather than to him: "He knew that his mother had been talking to Vera and Buddy about him, telling them that if he got into any more trouble he would be sent to prison" (15). This reduction of Bigger Thomas to the status of an object is taken up again in the confrontation between Wright's marginal hero and the macrocosm "American society": "The next morning they woke him, fed him, and took him back to court" (441).

The text reflects the protagonist's double consciousness and subject-object function by limiting the narrative to Bigger's point of view. At the same time, Bigger's emotional world is interpreted on an omniscient level:

> Bigger was afraid of robbing a white man and he knew that Gus was afraid, too. . . . [H]e had transferred his fear of the whites to Gus.   (27)

Whereas passages such as "Bigger was afraid of robbing a white man and he knew that Gus was afraid, too" belong to the figural perspective, describing the events from Bigger's point of view, phrases such as "he had transferred his fear of the whites to Gus" belong to a metalevel on which the narrator objectifies Bigger through sociopsychological explanations. This double perspective mirrors the conflict raging in the mind of the protagonist, who remains trapped between autonomy (Bigger as subject) and heteronomy (Bigger as object).

The contradictory use of recurrent moments of existential freedom and determinism, which is often criticized in studies on Richard Wright, should be seen as an artistic strength rather than as a weakness of the novel. It underpins the ambivalence of Bigger's search for an identity in a world that is not only psychologically but also culturally double-encoded: "He felt that he had his destiny in his grasp. He was more alive than he could ever remember having been" (170); "All his life he had been knowing that sooner or later something like this would come to him" (255). Such alternation between freedom and determinism accompanies Bigger's struggle for a discourse of his own throughout the novel.

My undergraduate students too often interpret the protagonist as an object-victim without considering his development as a subject striving for self-realization and self-expression: "At several points in the novel, Bigger tells about his inability to take action, to do things. This inability doesn't originate in Bigger's person being too stupid, but in the bad conditions under which he lives, the domination of the whites and Bigger's reduction to his own Waste Land" (Schaudt 6).

This unequivocal focus on objectification and victimization also characterizes my students' interpretation of the female characters in Wright's works: "A general indictment of women is expressed in Richard Wright's works" (Macke 7). This judgment corresponds to the view of the canon of feminist studies on

Native Son (see J. Davis; France; Harris; Mootry; Warren; S. Williams). However, what Alan W. France rightly identifies as a misogynist subtext in *Native Son*, the symbolic "feminization" and rape of Gus by Bigger in the poolroom scene (42–43; France 416–17), deconstructs itself. The marginalization of and violence against women in the novel are not delineated for their own sake but reflect the marginalization of the male protagonist, whose experience of oppression is also represented metaphorically through sexual imagery. Bigger's descriptions of Chicago convey phallic associations. Before Bigger's eyes towers a white world of steel, almost mechanical in its precision, and its illusory promises figuratively penetrate the minds of Bigger Thomas and the black community: "He blinked and the world grew hard again, mechanical, distinct" (16); "the vast white world that sprawled and towered in the sun before them" (18–19); "Every time I think about [white folks' not letting us do *nothing*] I feel like somebody's poking a red-hot iron down my throat" (20). Bigger's arrest toward the end of "Flight" can be interpreted not only as a symbolic crucifixion but also as the rape of a black rebel by the dominant white patriarchy: ". . . he was in the snow, lying flat on his back. . . . Two men stretched his arms out, as though about to crucify him; they placed a foot on each of his wrists, making them sink deep down in the snow" (314).

Despite the violence Bigger inflicts on women in *Native Son*, his destiny proves inseparably linked with the destiny of the novel's female characters. The two sides of Bessie Mears, whose surname metaphorically predestines her to serve as a reflector, mirrors Bigger's double consciousness: "there were two Bessies" (159). By killing her, Bigger symbolically kills the passive, negative side of his character and, metonymically, the passivity of the black community. In his nightmare, the severed head of Mary Dalton is a symbol of his self-decapitation: "it was his *own* head" (189). The death of Mary Dalton is tantamount to his inevitable end (102–03). The brutal violation of Bessie foreshadows his brutal subjugation by the white majority. Again, many students tend to overlook the metaphorical subtext of the novel, limiting their analysis to the surface level: "In the end [Bigger] kills [Bessie] because he had told her about the murder of Mary Dalton and for that reason he cannot leave her behind anymore. . . . Therefore in his eyes killing her is the logical conclusion" (Lampert 3).

The parallels between the marginalization of women and the marginalization of the black male protagonist in *Native Son* are obvious. In a world determined by hatred and violence, racism and sexism, a "separate peace" between the sexes turns out to be as utopian as the marginal hero's longing for recognition by and integration in mainstream society.

My students' failure to recognize the intricate blues syntax encoding the process of Bigger's self-articulation becomes understandable when one considers the preconceptions European undergraduates have about language, preconceptions that shed light on the educational framework in which they study. The emphasis placed on Standard English or High German in the white Western tradition leads students to ignore the fact that Black English is a distinct language system with "definite language patterns, syntax, grammar, and history" (Judge Charles Joiner qtd. in Wolfram 10). Many students interpret Black English as a sign of poor education or even a lack of intelligence: "The Daltons' language is highly educated, whereas the Black English of Reverend Hammond is absolutely uneducated" (Schuhmacher 4); "[Bessie] speaks the typical black English but is quite intelligent" (Lampert 3). Equally remarkable is that German undergraduates usually interpret the text's double meaning in terms of images familiar to them from white Western culture: "Another example of allusion and double meaning is the scene where Bigger carries the trunk with Mary's body downstairs. The reader gets the impression of Jesus Christ carrying his cross up to the hills of Golgotha whereas Bigger carries his cross down—to hell—to face his end" (Schuhmacher 20). Wright's "signifying upon" the black cultural tradition (see Gates Jr., *Signifying Monkey*) is not perceived as a possible intertextual paradigm.

With such preconceptions, it is no wonder that subtle strategies like Bigger's process of articulation in the subtext of *Native Son* remain unnoticed. The beginning of Bigger's development of an individual if still muffled voice can be detected in his response to texts enhancing the power of the dominant white discourse. The sentence "YOU CAN'T WIN!" (13) on the poster advertising Buckley's election campaign is undermined by Wright's marginal protagonist, who sees the reality of public corruption hidden behind the text: "He snuffed his cigarette and laughed silently. 'You crook,' he mumbled, shaking his head. 'You let whoever pays *you* off win!'" (13).

After the death of Mary Dalton, which constitutes Bigger's "act of *creation*" (466), Bigger succeeds more and more in manipulating the dominant discourse. He starts using his voice consciously and checks its effect on third parties: "He wondered just how his words *really* did sound. Was the tone of his voice this morning different from other mornings? Was there something unusual in his voice since he had killed Mary?" (114–15). Gradually, he is able to play with stereotypes and expectations prevalent in white society and to construct his own story: "Bigger knew the things that white folks hated to hear Negroes ask for" (225). In book 3, "Fate," it seems as if Bigger Thomas relapses into the voicelessness and passivity that characterized him before: "He simply lay or sat, saying nothing" (315). But a complex subtext reveals his increasing autonomy and puts into question John McCluskey's opinion about the irrelevance of the blues-jazz tradition in *Native Son*. Near the beginning of book 3, a syntactical structure leaps to the eye; it consists of a series of parallel participle clauses building up tension, finally to be resolved by a short independent clause. This structure has been identified by Joyce Ann Joyce as "periodic sentence construction" ("Style" 112–13):

> Having been thrown by an accidental murder into a position where he had sensed a possible order and meaning in his relations with the people about him; having accepted the moral guilt and responsibility for that

murder because it had made him feel free for the first time in his life;
having felt in his heart some obscure need to be at home with people . . .
having done all this and failed, he chose not to struggle any more.   (316)

This syntax, based on the traditionally tripartite structure of the blues (e.g.,
three blue notes, three phrases, three harmonies), regenerates Bigger's voice
and increasingly influences the language of the text as well as the characterization of the protagonist:

He lay on the cold floor sobbing; but really he was standing up strongly
with contrite heart, holding his life in his hands. . . . He lay on the cold floor
sobbing; but really he was pushing forward with his puny strength. . . . He
lay on the cold floor sobbing; but really he was groping forward with fierce
zeal. . . .   (359)

The blues syntax is then taken up by Bigger's Jewish American lawyer Boris
Max ("if we can encompass the life of this man . . . if we can understand . . . if we
can do this, perhaps we shall find the key to our future . . ." [444]) and is finally
perverted by the representative of the dominant society, state attorney Buckley:

My voice may sound harsh when I say: *Impose the death penalty and let
the law take its course.* . . . But I am really merciful and sympathetic. . . .
My voice may sound vindictive when I say: *Make the defendant pay the
highest penalty for his crimes!* But what I am really saying is that the law
is sweet when it is enforced. . . . My voice may sound cruel when I say:
The defendant merits the death penalty. . . . But what I am really saying
is that the law is strong and gracious. . . .   (475–76)

The process of articulation eventually leads to a situation of bitter irony.
Through his experience of marginality Bigger Thomas has been able to develop a new personal identity. Nevertheless he continues to be isolated, and his
message is not understood by the people surrounding him, even Max: "Max
groped for his hat like a blind man" (501).

The deictic relativity of inside and outside in *Native Son* has been ignored
by both literary critics and the undergraduate students who attended my seminar. Whereas German students have no problem perceiving and understanding the "chasm between the white and the black race" as delineated in *Native
Son* (Nelles 9), they frequently neglect the fact that Bigger Thomas is strongly
influenced by white patterns of thought and behavior. Bigger's response to the
movie *Trader Horn* shows the extent of his internalization of dominant values
and blurs the inside-outside binary that has long been used to simplify the
analysis of marginality in black texts:

He looked at *Trader Horn* unfold and saw pictures of naked black men
and women whirling in wild dances and heard drums beating and then

gradually the African scene changed and was replaced by images in his own mind of white men and women dressed in black and white clothes, laughing, talking, drinking and dancing. Those were smart people; they knew how to get hold of money, millions of it.   (36–37)

Three examples show Wright's improvisation on the phenomenon of deictic ambiguity, which has been examined by Karl Bühler and Roman Jakobson and formulated by Barbara E. Johnson in the following terms: "To be a subject means to activate the network of discourse from *where one stands*" (Response 43).

In the first example, the text plays with the ambivalent deixis of personal pronouns and thereby undermines the dominant social group's tendency to depersonalize the individual by means of simplistic categorizations: "'The last colored man who worked for us stayed ten years.' Bigger wondered why [Peggy] said 'us.' . . . 'Mr. Dalton's a fine man,' Peggy said. . . . 'You know, he does a lot for your people.' 'My people?' asked Bigger, puzzled" (62–63).

The second and third examples destabilize the inside-outside binary by foregrounding the ambiguity of spatial perspectives. In the following passage, Bigger attempts to express his experience of marginality metaphorically: "We live here and they live here. We black and they white. . . . It's just like living in jail. Half the time I feel like I'm on the outside of the world peeping in through a knot-hole in the fence. . . ." (20). Paradoxically, the images Bigger uses contain two different points of view. Jail implies his being inside a restricted area, looking out on a world beyond reach, whereas peeping through a knothole implies his being outside, looking in on a society that exiled him from its social life. The complexity of Wright's deconstruction of spatial categories in *Native Son* is revealed especially in passages where the protagonist is reduced to a marginal voyeur:

He squeezed through and stood in the snow on the roof. . . . Directly below him, one floor away, through a window without shades, he saw a room in which were two small iron beds with sheets dirty and crumpled. In one bed sat three naked black children looking across the room to the other bed on which lay a man and a woman, both naked and black in the sunlight.   (285–86)

Here, Bigger hides outside the black community; in a hostile white world symbolized by snow imagery, he witnesses the poverty and misery of everyday life inside the black neighborhood. Although he is part of the culture he observes, his perspective is that of a critical outsider influenced by the value system of a society to which he does not belong.

In view of the early reception of *Native Son*, it is not surprising that white undergraduate students interpret Bigger Thomas exclusively as a representative of the black community and accept at face value stereotypes that the novel presents ironically. Although—or perhaps precisely because—*Native Son* makes the lack of mutual understanding and communication between the races its central theme, the novel has long been misunderstood and misinterpreted. Literary critics and authors like James Baldwin and Ralph Ellison accused Wright of creating a protagonist who is not representative of the black community. They react as the black workers Jack and Jim did in *Native Son*. Bigger overhears Jack say: "tha' Goddamn nigger Bigger Thomas . . . made the white folks think we's *all* jus' like him!" (291). A literary character such as Bigger, whose thoughts and emotions are determined by the values and social control mechanisms of the dominant white society and whose behavior is virtually a projection of white expectations, can of course not be a representative of black culture. Bigger's importance is derived, rather, from his borderline position between two cultural traditions, both beyond his reach, and from the unwillingness of either to accept him as an individual.

Native Son continues to appeal to a new generation of readers, who are fascinated primarily by the novel's thrilling and eventful plot. "For the reader Wright's message is very sad. It is touching to understand that Bigger . . . has been given only little time to live a life that others lived" (Mancino 12). For this new generation of readers to comprehend and appreciate the complexity of Wright's masterpiece, however, either-or approaches to *Native Son* in teaching and research have to give way to a careful analysis of the novel's narrative text and subtexts. Ideally, students should be inspired to respond creatively to John Edgar Wideman's call for openness in literary criticism on black texts:

> One crucial step may be recognizing that black/white, either/or perceptions of the tensions within language are woefully inadequate. Start by taking nothing for granted, giving nothing away. Study the language. . . . Unveil the chaos within the patterns of certainty. Restate issues and paradigms so they are not simply the old race problem relexified.
>
> (Preface ix)

Literacy and the Liberation of Bigger Thomas
Melba Joyce Boyd

On 9 February 1992, family, friends, scholars, and writers gathered in Paris at 14 rue Monsieur-le-Prince to dedicate a commemorative plaque at the home of Richard Wright. People of every race and from the four corners of the Earth formed a meridian circle in tribute to this American writer. Misty-eyed, we stood in the rain without umbrellas, testifying and singing spirituals for this black American writer who endured racism, poverty, and even persecution by the United States government. His literature had profoundly influenced each of our lives and had substantially radicalized the reading of black America and the quest for freedom.

Richard Wright, who illuminated the intricacies of American hegemony in his fiction and nonfiction, has given us critical insight into the most horrible reaches of the American psyche. His novel *Native Son* reveals how racial hysteria consciously and subconsciously controls and manipulates the behavior and beliefs of most Americans. The continuing social and economic crisis for blacks and Latinos and Latinas in the United States demonstrates the catastrophic ramifications of racism and the need for a political pedagogy that can honestly address the repression that enshrouds those communities. Wright's prophetic novel is essential literature for their survival and reeducation.

The teaching of *Native Son* to a contemporary urban classroom should be contextualized within the historical parallels in and between the novel and the disparities of today. The reading of Bigger Thomas's character is especially significant during these critical times in American cities, even more so than in the 1940s, when the novel was first published, because Bigger's psychology is characteristic of a burgeoning profile in urban communities. Denied a meaningful education or gainful employment, Bigger Thomas has today fallen prey to the illegal economy of the drug trade. The media's celebration of materialism and the devaluation of human life in social and political programs has conditioned him to seek status and wealth as quickly as possible. The anger and hatred he feels is greater than his fear of death. And because he doesn't believe he has a future, he doesn't care about his history. He expects a fast and dangerous life and a premature death.

There aren't any Bigger Thomases among my students at Wayne State University, because literacy has defined their aspirations and social conditions, as illiteracy or nonliteracy defined those of Wright's character. However, many of my students are related to him, and many of them will be in a position to teach and possibly avert the social pathology of potential Biggers. At the same time, the study of *Native Son* not only informs those who have escaped Bigger's fate but also reveals how they may be afflicted by the ignorance or arrogance that perpetuates and executes racist ideology. This blindness affects judgment, distorts perception, and restricts intelligence. When done in keeping with the thematic principles outlined by Wright, the teaching of *Native Son* involves a moral lesson for us all. As educators it is our responsibility to change the way society and its institutions instill inhumane beliefs and perpetuate discrimination. *Native Son* not only identifies the consequences of racial oppression, it also illuminates the cultural thought that encourages inequities, hatred, and the myth of Caucasian supremacy.

Any reading of *Native Son* has to include a discussion of Wright's essay "How Bigger Was Born." This essay explains how Wright's fictional character is drawn from a myriad of real persons Wright knew and from their responses to oppressive conditions. "Almos' a Man" is also immensely useful in the teaching of *Native Son*. The short story provides a historical foreground for the novel and a direct correlation between two characters who embrace the American mythology of violence as a venue for social power and respect.

Unless given the skills and the passion to cultivate their minds and spirits, Bigger Thomases will continue to be reborn at a phenomenal rate into the future. For this reason, *Native Son* should be taught to all American students, but especially to students of color. The novel gives a serious critique of America's deprived historical and social conscience; it argues that this country must face its ugliness if its citizens are ever to resolve their national moral crisis.

The Films in the Novel

It is clear from the novel that Wright identifies Hollywood as a major force in the intensification of stereotypes and the perpetuation of racial illusions in American culture and society. Insofar as this approach to teaching *Native Son* recognizes the contemporary culture of the student as a part of the learning experience, it also acknowledges the impact of the visual culture on the students' perception of themselves and others. Likewise, the details and the intricacies of Bigger's world and Bigger's imagination have been seriously injured by the cinema. When Bigger goes to the movie house, he views two different films which contain the same ideological perspective: one that glamorizes bourgeois decadence, degrades social and political dissidence, and perpetuates Caucasian supremacy and upper-class privilege. Bigger bitterly internalizes the films' inherent cultural myths. The films reinforce his hatred of himself and his desire for the luxurious world that is verboten. This view and these feelings are exchanged in a wishful commentary with his friend Jack:

> "I'd like to be invited to a place like that just to find out what it feels like," Bigger mused.
> "Man, if them folks saw you they'd run," Jack said. "They'd think a gorilla broke loose from the zoo and put on a tuxedo." ([1966] 33)

During the ending of the film *The Gay Woman*, as the adulterous wife regains her affection for her husband and they vow to live happily ever after, the remarks of Bigger and Jack reveal their perception of the movie as documentation of a reality:

> "You reckon folks really act like that?" Bigger asked, full of the sense of a life he had never seen.
> "Sure, man. They rich," Jack said. . . .
> "Shucks. I got a great mind to take that job," Bigger said.
> "Sure. You don't know what you might see."
> They laughed. Bigger turned his eyes to the screen, but he did not look. He was filled with a sense of excitement about his new job. Was what he heard about rich white people really true? Was he going to work for people like you saw in the movies? ([1966] 35)

Bigger's mind wanders, musing with hopeful anticipation about his encounter with his rich white employers while barbaric images of Africans dance on the screen from the film *Trader Horn*. By activating myths about poor whites to bolster his class status, Bigger convinces himself that his dream can be realized. Grasping at a remote newspaper report of a black chauffeur's fairy-tale marriage to his young white mistress, Bigger even envisions himself in a relationship with the rich daughter. He configures a world like a Hollywood movie, one that does not exist and will not appear in the future. This daydream, built on castles of sand evoked by the cinema, provides an enticing escape from his black reality.

But what Bigger will experience in his future relationship with the young heiress is not derived from the cinematic daydreams. Mary associates with Communists, who are cast as villains in *The Gay Woman*, and what she wants to offer Bigger is friendship, not sex; equality, not money. Neither of these communist ideals inhabits Bigger's dreams, because in the absence of a political consciousness the popular culture and a vicious economy have effectively instilled material wealth and sexual prowess as admirable traits or as compensation for self-respect and freedom. Bigger's historical ignorance and displaced imagination render him desperate prey for a racist society; more important, his racial fear and hysteria render him disastrous.

Black-White, White-Black: Beyond Two-Dimensional Thought

The simplistic, two-dimensional imagery refracted in the movies constitutes the social fabric that contains everything and everybody in the black-white conflict. Wright inverts this framework, extending the literal, linear reading of social symbolism by piercing the illusion and reaching for the truth that resides in the image inside the image. In other words, symbolic language reveals the implications and intentions behind what the characters think and do. "Fear" is the organic center of the novel, and as the story unfolds, the symbolic dimensions of book 1 become manifest. Wright's black-and-white motif contains the contradiction present at the beginning of the novel. But too often students, like the characters in the novel, are so conditioned by the illusion and abuse of language that unless the structural and symbolic elements in the text are pointed out to them, they won't recognize the obvious and certainly not the oblique.

In the opening scene, for instance, the rat, Bigger, Mrs. Thomas, and Bigger's brother are all identified as black. A point of contrast is Vera, Bigger's sister, who is described as brown. This is the first sign that black is not a racial or descriptive feature in Wright's narrative but rather a social designation that indicates doom and defeat. In fact, the rat chase foreshadows Bigger's ultimate fate. While desperately fighting for some living space, the rat is personified, whereas Bigger is dehumanized when he fights for his life and the white world hunts him down like an animal and characterizes him as an ape. Both the rat and Bigger are doomed even before they begin their struggle.

White or whiteness also has a social and psychological effect on Bigger and other black people. It correlates with death and blindness and is associated with arrogance and insensitivity. Bigger finds comfort and shelter in the darkness, whereas whiteness threatens and entraps him. The ghostlike figure of Mrs. Dalton epitomizes this symbolic code, and as the novel progresses, the police encloses the black community like the engulfing snowstorm. The newspaper map reflects the white force that surrounds and shrinks Bigger's black space. The weather forecasts Bigger's inevitable doom, while the black-and-white print of the paper outlines and justifies this encroachment of pale death.

Because these symbolic cues are often decoded by the students matter-of-factly, it is essential that these signs are identified or else the metaphorical level of seeing escapes their reading. The meaning behind the cues, like the subtle signs of institutional racism, goes unnoticed. At best it is encoded on a subliminal level.

In the historical reality of these cues, whiteness is a force of repression for black people in general, and in *Native Son*, it is a symbol of death for Bigger in particular. Just as the newspaper is used by the Thomases to cover the bloody corpse of the rat, Bigger's fatal end is largely due to the newspaper reports that condemn and dehumanize him. A significant point to make in the teaching of literature and literacy is that the media, audiovisual and print, should not be perceived as "the truth"; rather, the media speaks in the language and from the perspective of institutions of control. A critical imagination must understand the structural and philosophical parameters of that order to challenge it. To be able to see the intentions and ramifications of cultural and social hegemony is a major thematic purpose of Wright's novel. It is essential that students realize that they cannot believe everything they read and that their intuitive intelligence and common sense must be engaged in the deciphering of so-called objectivity.

Indeed, the "professionals," the learned psychiatrist and the university sociologist who purport theories about black inferiority to help convict Bigger, represent the broader psychology of institutional racism that still persists in current popular beliefs about black people. For example, the controversial 1965 "Moynihan Report" (named after its author, the then Harvard professor Daniel Patrick Moynihan, it found the deterioration of the black family to be the fundamental cause of weakness in the black community) has given significant authority to the blaming of female-headed households for juvenile delinquency in the black community. But this "scientific" study ignores unemployment and social repression, the real root causes for the past and present problems of black youth.

Ironically, the institutions that have the resources and power to address those problems generally go uncriticized for their repressive abuse of black people, and the prevailing rhetoric, which calls for black male role models, has been embraced by most black professionals and community leaders. The absence of a class analysis has allowed a racist, sexist hegemony to mislead and confuse people's perception of reality, so that they have no clear understanding of the source and force of crime and violence in the black community. None of the reputable experts and community leaders correlate the emulation of violent, sexist, rich white male role models who star in films, and who initiate and conduct wars, with the destructive behavior of young black men who have gone awry.

Burning Social Issues

A more obvious parallel between Wright's novel and American history is the recent resurgence of the Ku Klux Klan. The KKK has consistently been one of the most blatant manifestations of racial hatred in the history of anti-Americanism. The destructive force of this undemocratic organization is celebrated in America's best-selling novel of all time, *Gone with the Wind*, which demonstrates the romanticism associated with racial terrorism. To obscure the severity of racism in our society is a serious mistake, because the tolerance or the intolerance of this evil seems to be an indicator of the liberalism or illiberalism of the larger society.

The 1991 Louisiana gubernatorial campaign of David Duke, an ex-Klansman and founder of the National Association for the Advancement of White People, was based on bigotry as a political strategy and as a social proclivity. And for a striking example of how the racist hysteria portrayed in *Native Son* has been refracted in the contemporary American imagination, we need only recall the notorious Willie Horton episode of the 1988 presidential campaign. Criminal images of black men still dominate the national racial discourse.

The failure of our educational institutions to teach Americans out of their socialized ignorance and wickedness has encouraged and perpetuated the myth of Caucasian supremacy. The burning of the cross in front of Bigger's jail by the KKK is a crucifixion scene, and this image has haunted black American literature and life since the era of Reconstruction.

The Film Native Son

Just as the cinema is a part of the novel, the film *Native Son* (the 1986 version) should be a part of the teaching of the novel. In a key scene, the director craftfully frames Bigger in a black-white image that contextualizes Bigger's physical and psychological entrapment as well as his fate. Conceptually reflexive, Bigger's imprisonment is penetrated by a black shadow that cuts across the white cell wall and across his body caught in the vortex. The abstractness of the black-white imagery in the film provides thematic insight. The use of scenes like this from the film in the teaching of the novel illustrates how conceptual dimensions can be expressed through the language of visual symbols. It is also important to realize that the cinema that affects Bigger's imagination contains the same historical imagery that has impacted on the imagination of students in the classroom.

The inclusion of film in the teaching of the novel provides an opportunity to integrate visual literacy with reading. Students need to know how film works; otherwise they will be victimized by cultural technology. Through critical examination they can consider how the film *Native Son* both counters and extends the popular culture. Discussion of films like *Boyz in the Hood* and *Almos' a Man* (based on the Wright story) should also be considered in the context of literature and literacy.

The teaching of *Native Son* is an attempt to liberate the imagination and to advance critical, social thought. Bigger Thomas is a native son, an indigenous American character whose identity and fate were shaped by forces beyond his perception and control. It was not some ethereal agency that sent Bigger to an early grave but, rather, the social and economic ravages of capitalist greed, capitalism's corruption of the American imagination, and the fear and the hatred capitalism invokes by dividing communities and classes into colors and defining human beings with vicious stereotypes.

It is a difficult task to teach disfranchised Americans to transcend the contradictions of their condition while inhumane economic and social policies repeatedly plague and assault them. But contemporary African American students—like Richard Wright, a poor black boy who had the nerve to evolve above and beyond the gravity of tragedy and the insult of popular ignorance and abuse—represent the promise for change in the classroom and in the cities. Understanding why Bigger Thomas suffers will help them develop the imagination and fortitude that will change this diabolical democracy. With critical insight grounded in reality and with a creative language forged into an alternative vision, they will use the liberation of Bigger Thomas as the leverage that frees America from the dichotomy of its racial hysteria. Enlightenment can come only from those who have learned to see through the dark and into the light.

> Another impulse rose in him, born of desperate need, and his mind
> clothed it in an image of a strong blinding sun sending hot rays down and

he was standing in the midst of a vast crowd of men, white men and black men and all men, and the sun's rays melted away the many differences, the colors, the clothes, and drew what was common and good upward toward the sun. . . .   (335)

Native Son as Project

Laura L. Quinn

I have taught *Native Son* in classes on the American novel or the modern novel; in introductory literature classes; in an African American survey course titled Alternative Traditions in American Literature; and, finally, in a seminar on Langston Hughes, Zora Neale Hurston, and Richard Wright. I find it increasingly difficult to teach this important novel in the general American literature course or in the genre course. The enthusiasm and the resistance that it generates in my students seem irremediably problematic when my students have no knowledge of African American literary history and therefore no sense of the kind of project that *Native Son* was for Richard Wright. The novel needs to be historicized in particular ways, ways that are unmanageable (for me, at least) in an American literature or novels course dominated by white authors. I have, however, had more success with this approach in a specifically structured introductory literature class.

Teaching *Native Son* at a small, expensive liberal arts college in western Pennsylvania, I generally encounter the highest level of enthusiasm for the text among white male students and the highest level of resistance from white female students, especially those with a nascent or developed feminist consciousness. My African American students (anywhere between three percent to thirty percent of a given class) tend to be middle-class high achievers for whom Bigger Thomas is an embarrassment, though these students are often the most interested in exploring what Wright is about in his representation of this difficult character. While I am not always clear (but always anxious) about why the white male students like the novel (I am certain they are not clear about it themselves), I can catalog the kinds of resistance I encounter among a variety of students:

> Bigger's criminality, his violence are impossible for students to romanticize (I hope my white male students are not excepted here) and often difficult for them to understand at any level, given their mostly privileged backgrounds.
>
> The Daltons are probably the most recognizable representations in the novel for my students. Philanthropic slumlords who are guilty of innocence (at best) about American race relations are not indictable within the value systems students bring to the novel. The Daltons' victimization is likely to get more attention than their culpability does.
>
> The end of the cold war may render anticommunism less virulent in my students' generation, but it certainly makes figures like Jan Erlone and Boris Max seem aggravatedly obsolete and incomprehensible to them.
>
> The novel's misogyny throws up a wall to self-consciously feminist students.
>
> The literary education my students bring to the novel is still grounded in a New Critical formalism that resists "politics" in literature and that will accept automatically those critical responses that claim failure for the third part of *Native Son*.
>
> My students—particularly African American and women students—have often developed the kind of critical consciousness that calls for "image control" in cultural products; and there are no characters in this novel whose images they find acceptable.

Despite all the above, the novel is a powerful and unsettling reading experience for almost all students. Teachers need to mediate that reading experience by having students interact with the historical complexities of the novel's production and reception. Given the time constraints of the classroom, I have found three course-specific approaches productive.

In the African American historical survey course, students will have systematically studied white control over and appropriation of African American cultural products, beginning with slave narratives that are ghostwritten or transcribed or introduced by whites. Matters of black-white cultural relations and the question of black-white symbiosis (a vestige of plantation-culture paternalism) continue to appear through the late nineteenth century and early twentieth in works like *Autobiography of an Ex-Colored Man* (1912). The Harlem Renaissance, of course, raises such issues richly when figures like Carl Van Vechten, Mrs. Rufus Osgood Mason, Fanny Hurst, and Nancy Cunard are studied alongside the black artists and writers who had such complex and varied interactions with them. In this historical context Wright's "Blueprint for Negro Writing," which appeared in the *New Challenge* in 1937 and which begins with a biting indictment of "prim and decorous ambassadors who went a'begging to white America" (37), can begin to illuminate the project of *Native Son*. I like to pair this piece with Du Bois's 1935 essay "A Negro Nation within the Nation" to suggest to students (already familiar with Du Bois as the author of *The Souls of Black Folk*, the editor of *Crisis*, and luminary of the Harlem Renaissance) that the turn to black nationalism that Wright concerns himself with in "Blueprint" is historically situated and a reaction to the Harlem Renaissance's cultural utopianism. The other crucial gloss to the production of *Native Son* is of course "How Bigger Was Born," particularly the paragraph on *Uncle Tom's Children*, in which Wright admits his mistake in writing "a book which even bankers' daughters could read and weep over and feel good about" (531). Understanding that Bigger was born not just out of Wright's experience but also out of Wright's felt need to take African American literature in a new direction in its relation to a white public moves students beyond their desire to see the novel as unmediated coarse reality and brings them to a sense of the novel's historical self-consciousness. In addition, their increased understanding of the politics of literary production enables them to move beyond the formalist position that devalues Wright's novel as political.

Just when the students think they know what materials and moments gave birth to Bigger, teachers should unsettle them with some history of the novel's reception, its Book-of-the-Month Club status and its immediate popularity. The new, uncut Library of America edition makes it possible for me to read aloud to a class a few of the deletions requested by the editor—notably the Regal Theater masturbation scene and the scene in Mary Dalton's bedroom. (It is interesting that students often focus on what this kind of editorial intervention meant rather than on their own reactions to a more explicit representation of Bigger's sexuality.) Wright's complicity with his editor's request is the first of a series of maneuvers to soften the rawness of Bigger Thomas's story. I tell my students of the 1941 stage version of the novel, written by Wright and Paul Green, in which the Bessie Mears character—now Clara Mears—is killed by a police bullet while Bigger shields himself with her body; in the novel she is beaten with a brick by Bigger and stuffed down an airshaft to freeze to death. I describe the 1986 film version (for which, of course, Wright has no responsibility), in which Bessie is not killed at all and Mary Dalton's head simply dangles outside the furnace briefly before Bigger is able to stuff it in, obviating the need to behead her with a hatchet. The evisceration of the story's violence and sexuality, combined with its continuing representational appeal, leads to lively discussions of what kinds of cultural work *Native Son* seems to be able to do. We frequently return to the text to consider the uses to which Bigger is put in a racist culture, the uses made of the bodies of Bessie Mears and (what's left of) Mary Dalton, and the uses that we as readers today are making of this novel.

In studying the novel's reception, we also consider the responses of Ralph Ellison and James Baldwin to *Native Son*, particularly the emphasis of both on Bigger as a representation of a white version of black humanity (or, more accurately, subhumanity). Having students read "Richard Wright's Blues" from Ellison's *Shadow and Act* and "Many Thousands Gone" from Baldwin's *Notes of a Native Son* has occasionally backfired for me: students, swept up by the articulate lyricism of these critiques, uncritically accepted them, and their acceptance closed off the dialogue about *Native Son*. But if students see that Wright's novel is a self-conscious project of representation, it becomes possible for them to situate historically the strong responses of Ellison and Baldwin and to explore what might have been at stake for the two as African American writers in the mid-forties and early fifties, given *Native Son*'s popular reception. When the trajectory of an African American representational dilemma is thus plotted, students become able to view their own complex responses to the novel metacritically and with interest. They return to the text and write about it—now even from a formalist or structural perspective—with more critical distance and greater respect for Wright's artistic-political commitment.

In the seminar I teach on Hughes, Hurston, and Wright, I do not have the historical breadth of the survey course to bring to bear on our reading of *Native Son*, but I have the countervailing opportunity to assign more of Wright's other writing. We read *Black Boy, American Hunger, Uncle Tom's Children,* and *The Outsider*. Many of the seminar students are reading *Native Son* for a second time and are ready to approach it in sophisticated ways. I assign two essays from the collection *Major Literary Characters: Bigger Thomas,* edited by Harold Bloom, both of which address the problem of narrative voice in the novel. In her essay, Laura E. Tanner claims that the narrative voice disempowers Bigger linguistically:

> To rewrite Bigger's thoughts within a secure and sophisticated linguistic framework is in some sense to distort the nature of his thoughts, founded as they are in the consciousness of a man whose problematic relationship to the master language defines his very identity.   (131)

Valerie Smith, in her essay, claims that the free indirect discourse Wright employs in the novel does enable Bigger to find a voice. This dialogue enables seminar students to test their responses to Bigger's voiced or voiceless presence in the novel. The choice that Wright made regarding voice in the novel can also be compared with the use of vernacular in the work of Hughes and in Hurston's *Their Eyes Were Watching God* (in Hurston's novel free indirect discourse is also prominent). This formalist concern broadens into a consideration of the politics behind each author's choice of voice; we read Hughes's essay "The Negro Artist and the Racial Mountain," Hurston's essay "How It Feels to Be Colored Me," and, again, "Blueprint for Negro Writing" to set these statements of artistic purpose against the works that enact the statements. What emerges from this examination is that voice seems to be a far less crucial element in *Native Son* than it is in Hurston's novel, Hughes's poems, or Hughes's novel *Not without Laughter*. Voice does not seem to be the source of *Native*

Son's power. We find that source, rather, in the novel's scene-making capacity, in the elaboration of such moments as the rat-killing opener, the arduous movement up the stairs with drunken Mary Dalton to her bedroom and her death, that very long interval with the gentleman of the press in the furnace room when the burnt body is discovered, Bigger's capture on the roof, and the family reunion or gathering at the police station that culminates in Bigger's shame and rage as his mother kneels before Mrs. Dalton. Bigger is delivered to us not orally so much as visually or viscerally; the novel is cinematic rather than voiced.

This insight helps us account for the problems with book 3 ("Fate"). Tanner argues that the rhetoric of book 3 is a doubling of the narrative voice, that "Max functions in the plot exactly as the narrator's presence functions in the novel" (137). When *Native Son* is set against *Their Eyes Were Watching God*, we can see the error in this judgment. Janie's story in Hurston's novel—free indirect discourse notwithstanding—is being told to us, its voice a palpable presence. In book 3 of *Native Son*, Bigger's story is told by Max, by Buckley, by the newspapers that Bigger reads so eagerly—but each telling is quite different, each is alien to Bigger even as he is fascinated with being the subject of it. Much of what is powerful in "Fate" is the incongruity of Bigger's physical, mostly mute presence with the proliferation of voices and narratives that surround him. His effort to speak at the end of the novel meets only with Max's inability to respond to a man on the brink of death. The physicality, materiality, of Bigger is what is palpable and powerful in *Native Son*.

As fairly radical differences in the artistic practices of Hurston and Wright emerge in the seminar (with Hughes as a kind of fluid, mediating figure), I urge students to make use of the poetics and autobiographies of each author to account for those differences. *American Hunger* should be compared with "Blueprint for Negro Writing" to show the complexity and ambivalence of Wright's relation to Communism and to the politics of his craft. To provide a larger context for the issues to consider in the Hurston-Wright contest, I assign Hazel Carby's essay "Ideologies of Black Folk: The Historical Novel of Slavery." Though Carby refers only briefly to Hurston and Wright, her claim that African American urban writing is currently neglected in favor of a romanticized rural folk tradition is important to the study of *Native Son*. If voice and oral tradition are to be privileged discourses in the criticism of African American literature, Wright's contribution in *Native Son* will be undervalued. I want my seminar students to have a sense of how critical discourse is fashioned; that is, whatever their politics, I want them to know that literary reputation is a political phenomenon.

The final context in which I teach *Native Son* is the introductory literature course, which is required for all majors in our department and widely taken by nonmajors. It has a common-core structure: each section teaches a different approach to literature—formalist, historical, psychological, and feminist. We read a variety of short texts, but students are required to write four papers on one novel assigned for the course, each paper using one of the four approaches. *Native Son* is a splendid choice for this purpose, enabling students to learn the strengths and limitations of each approach. When introductory literature students are given prolonged and varied exposure to the novel, their experience of it will more likely be textured and complex. Students begin with the formalist paper, usually electing to write on a pattern or motif in the novel (e.g., whiteness), explicate a passage, or focus on structure. The historical paper requires research into American Communism in the thirties, the Scottsboro case, Loeb and Leopold, the Robert Nixon trial, and other contextualizing matters. The psychological paper requires research into psychological studies of race and racism and their applications to the novel. The feminist paper needs to avoid the obvious condemnation of the novel, so I ask them to develop a reply to that condemnation, a feminist defense of *Native Son*. Writing four papers on the same novel demands rereading and rethinking, the sort of work that *Native Son* deserves and rewards.

Because *Native Son* is an accessible text and a powerful and immediate reading experience, there is always the danger that its politics and artistry will seem transparent to student readers. To work against this tendency, teaching approaches must use recursive and intertextual strategies that build context around the book and keep bringing students back to their engagement with it.

Race and the Teaching of *Native Son*

Garrett H. White

Writing of W. E. B. Du Bois's prescient insight into the color line, John Edgar Wideman focuses our atttention on the obvious. "The color line raises the issue of identity. Theirs. Yours. Mine" (Introduction xiii). Wideman asserts simply and profoundly that we are all implicated in the color line; how we perceive and engage the color line contributes to our definition as individuals, as a community, and as a nation. With the publication of *Native Son*, Richard Wright boldly thrust his vision of part of that complex color line before the American public. Wideman's recognition of our personal and collective implication holds true for Wright's novel as well.

Native Son is about race. Despite Wright's discussion of white Biggers in "How Bigger Was Born," the most important fact about Bigger Thomas is his race, and the color line in all its complexity is the most important fact in the novel. Such statements may seem obvious and general, but they deserve a moment's reflection. I'm suggesting that when teaching *Native Son*, we would be wise to address the obvious with great care and that we can confront and employ race in our teaching very profitably.

Native Son absolutely defies a complacent response. In the introduction to *New Essays on* Native Son, Keneth Kinnamon reminds us of the "searing emotional force that gripped readers with and against their will" (19). The force is no doubt a function of the thrilling, sensational character of the story in the novel's first two books, but I think the novel derives the bulk of its power from Wright's unmerciful representation of racial conflict. And by conflict I mean not so much the crude bigotry illustrated by the newspaper clippings Wright composes as the more subtle clash of perspectives embodied so economically in the painfully awkward interaction of Mary, Jan, and Bigger.

Native Son turns on the tragic consequences of an encounter between white and black that is defined by ignorance and misperception. Jan and Mary's fateful night out with Bigger constitutes the crux of the plot and the heart of the novel. Readers have long recognized that Jan's sincere ambition to recruit Bigger for the Communist Party and Mary's well-intentioned desire to engage Bigger on some kind of social, friendly footing lead directly to the murder. John Reilly, in his afterword to the HarperPerennial 1966 edition of *Native Son*, calls attention to the significance of this plotting in two ways. First, he praises the novel's creativity by describing a "startling innovation in plot," Wright's inverting "the pitiable and familiar story of the black victim, making the Negro the violent attacker" (393). Wright forces the reader to confront race, to confront his perception of the color line, without the easy escape of sentiment. Bigger is cast against type as the violent attacker to subvert practiced sympathy on the part of his readers.

Reilly proceds to complicate our sense of what a victim is when he observes that the "description of Mary's murder makes clear that the white world is the cause of [Bigger's] violent desires and reactions" (395). Bigger may not be a stereotypical black victim, a narrative cliché, but he is most certainly a victim, of white America collectively and of Mary's and Jan's ignorance specifically. Mary and Jan's interest in getting to know Bigger is patronizing and self-serving. Their ignorance of this fact only amplifies the demeaning effect of their actions. The condescending treatment of Bigger is a function of their good intentions and of the blindness that informs and protects those intentions. Mary's and Jan's interest in Bigger may be genuine, but it remains superficial because Bigger is more black type to them than a complex individual, a rounded human being. They come to their relationship with him from a position of power, with knowledge that they presume to be superior to his. Their sense of themselves, of their identities, and of Bigger depends on a blindness that is ultimately quite willful. This willful blindness may be paradoxically unconscious, part of a culturally received epistemology, but it is nonetheless an important component of their personalities.

Their interest in Bigger centers on their appetite for the experience of eating at "one of those places where colored people eat" (69). They insinuate themselves into his life as boorish tourists for whom native cuisine is something novel and thrilling. Mary and Jan both use the leverage and power of their status as whites, and as employer's daughter and her friend, to make Bigger take them to Ernie's Kitchen Shack. They choose when and how to be friendly and social and when to treat Bigger as invisible black servant. That they on occasion do reach out and try to put him at ease only foregrounds the fact that they are forcing the encounter on him and can tailor it to their needs. They are remotely cognizant of his humanity only when it interests them or when his discomfort momentarily intrudes on their self-absorbed agenda. If forced to perceive Bigger as an individual who shares the same humanity, they would be forced to perceive their actions and attitudes as patronizing and self-serving; their identities would crumble.

The series of scenes leading up to and concluding with Mary's murder bear extraordinary significance; they express the complex of racial relations Wright intends to represent. In fact, one can make sense of the exquisitely detailed drama, the setting, the dialogue, the reactions, and of Bigger's state of mind only in terms of race first. Readers must acknowledge the color line to comprehend the physical and psychological action of the novel. Even if they can avoid implicating themselves personally in this color line, they cannot avoid confronting Wright's vision of a white race implicated communally and individually, responsible for Bigger's becoming a murderer. Reading and comprehending such scenes is indeed a searing experience.

Wright and many of his readers knew very well what was at stake in the plotting, characterization, symbolism, and other aspects of *Native Son*, even if they privileged one aspect over another or ignored some. David Cohn's rabid and contentious review of *Native Son* in the *Atlantic Monthly* and Wright's astute and pointed reply to it nicely isolate the issue that concerns me most, the stance one adopts toward *Native Son* and the implications and consequences of that positioning. Equally important is that this exchange shows Wright's aware-ness of the reader's participation in the novel. In his review, Cohn does more than reveal his inattentiveness to detail (Bigger's age) and condemn *Native Son* as "a blinding and corrosive study in hate" (57). He endeavors to construct an alternative vision of the color line that is at the same time Pollyannaish ("In all of the non-Southern states, Negroes have complete political rights") and deeply pessimistic ("The Negro problem in America is actually insoluble") (58, 61). He tries to present himself as a compassionate but superior and sanguine liberal in contrast to the hateful, hyperbolic, Communist Wright. Most important, he but-tresses his authority by invoking his Jewish birthright to a superior knowledge of oppression. Cohn describes Max as "a member of a race which has known something of oppression—not for three centuries, the length of the Negro's res-idence in America, but for more than twenty centuries in nearly every country of the world" (59). The rhetoric and incoherent logic of Cohn's polemic invites dissection, but I am not interested here in his specious reasoning, the imaginary historical and sociological analysis he offers, or the acrobatics he performs in the defense of a "tolerable" status quo. What matters is the stance he adopts con-sciously and unconsciously toward *Native Son* and the color line in general.

Wright zeroes in on Cohn's unsubtle maneuver in the second sentence of his reply:

> In the eyes of the average white American reader, [Cohn's] article made it more difficult for a Negro (child of slaves and savages!) to answer a cul-tured Jew (who had two thousand years of oppression to recommend him in giving advice to other unfortunates!) than an American white.   (62)

Wright succeeds, despite the awkward prose, in identifying both Cohn's adopted position of authority and the rationale behind it. Cohn wishes to reject any personal implication in the color line and to subvert Wright's analysis of the color line as insufficiently informed. But as much as Cohn wants to change the subject and silence Wright, he must first place himself in some kind of relation to the color line and confront race. Wright lays Cohn's gambit bare: "What alarms Mr. Cohn is not what I say Bigger *is*, but what I say *made* him what he is" (65). To preserve his own identity, Cohn must reject the idea that the white community bears responsibility. Deflecting Cohn's naive complaint that Wright did not understand that racial oppression warped whites as well as blacks, Wright observes that Cohn remains as blind to Bigger's humanity as the white characters in *Native Son*.

> The one piece of incriminating evidence which would have solved the "murder mystery" was Bigger's humanity, and the Daltons, Britten, and the newspaper men could not see or *admit* the living clue of Bigger's hu-manity under their very eyes!   (67; emphasis added)

At issue here is Wright's effort to force whites to admit the humanity of blacks and in that process admit their own place in and along the color line.

We must remember that all the abovementioned confronting of race is in response to the novel. The confronting that takes place in the novel takes place also in our experience of it during and after the act of reading. In experience, what matters is language and our apprehension of it. By apprehension I mean especially the intuitive, almost unconscious, component in comprehension, what E. H. Gombrich has identified as the beholder's share. Gombrich's concept of the "beholder's share in the reading of the artistic image" (182) is often and profitably transposed to the reader's constitutive role in literature. The beholder shares in the construction of meaning—using the knowledge, imagination, intuition, and schema that influence perception. The reader depends on past experience, particularly experience with language, to decipher and make sense of what is read. Much of that experience is received knowledge of collectively held opinions, values, expectations, and the schema (or patterns) of which Gombrich writes. In the essay "Giving Bigger a Voice: The Politics of Narrative in *Native Son*," Reilly is acutely aware of the beholder's share. Laying a foundation for his excellent study of Wright's narrative techniques in the novel, he describes a simple epistemology of reading: "[Unaware of] the weight of cultural baggage it carries, an audience comes to *Native Son* with experience in the field of discourse on blacks in America. . . . Readers enter the novel as though it were an entirely new treatment, while unconsciously bringing to bear on the narrative a fund of received lore." Reilly argues convincingly that Wright "meant to engage the patterns of received racial discourse" (35, 37, 60).

With his language and narration, Wright obliges readers to modify, according to the terms of the novel, their share in the construction of meaning. He compels them not only to confront how they perceive race and the color line but also to hear a voice and apprehend a perspective hitherto unknown to them. His innovations in plotting and character are meant to battle what Henry Louis Gates Jr. describes as the real "threat to the margin," "the homogenization of the other as, simply, the other" ("Studies" 298). In Reilly's terms, "Wright's intent . . . was to secure the right of a black to tell a black story," to validate and give voice to "black subjectivity" ("Giving" 60).

A focus on race in the reading experience of *Native Son* establishes a pedagogical approach flexible enough to be appropriate for a number of curricula. But teachers must have rhetorical dexterity and a willingness to investigate and modify their own posture toward the literature. For a model of such rhetorical dexterity, we can turn to Du Bois's exquisite paradigm of double consciousness:

> The Negro is sort of a seventh son, born with a veil, and gifted with second-sight in this American world,—a world which yields him no true self-consciousness, but only lets him see himself through the revelation of the other world. It is a peculiar sensation, this double-consciousness,

this sense of always looking at one's self through the eyes of others, of measuring one's soul by the tape of a world that looks on in amused contempt and pity.   (8)

Du Bois's model for African American identity is not a simple one. To be aware of the peculiar doubling he describes requires a higher level of consciousness. Perceiving oneself in the gaze of another results not just in one soul's being defined by that gaze and a second soul's striving to define itself but also in a third level of consciousness, which recognizes the inadequacy of the first two. One can attain Du Bois's double consciousness only from a perspective removed from it, aware of the "two souls; two thoughts; two unreconciled strivings; two warring ideals" (8). Teaching *Native Son* requires an analogous self-conscious awareness of the two conflicting perspectives in the novel and of the necessary vantage points from which to perceive them.

What teachers should avoid is an inhibiting white authentication of *Native Son* of the sort Robert Stepto has demonstrated to be an attribute of slave narratives (*Veil*) and Kinnamon (Introduction) has shown to be at work in *Native Son* and in Wright's relationships with his editor, Edward Aswell, and with Dorothy Canfield Fisher, who wrote the introduction to the first edition of the novel. Kinnamon describes the process of white authentication simply and well. To ensure a receptive white audience, "a well-known white abolitionist would provide a preface, guarantee, or letter attesting to the veracity or historicity of the narrative and the genuineness of the author's credentials." But an "authenticator's white perspective inevitably distorted as it mediated the necessarily different black perspective" (17). Many critics have discussed the limitations of Max's understanding of Bigger. Kinnamon goes further, arguing that Aswell "may even be regarded as standing in relation to Wright as Max stands in relation to Bigger: sympathetic, loyal, analytical, understanding to a point, but not quite ready to accept the full and uncut expression of a sensibility so radically different from his own" (16). Whether it is Max's pleading Bigger's case, Aswell's encouraging Wright to accede to the Book-of-the-Month Club's requests for revision, or Fisher's confused endorsement of *Native Son*, distortion is the result. Good intentions, whether of the authenticator or of Mary and Jan, encourage a false confidence in the acuity of one's perspective. The teacher can best mitigate if not avoid this pitfall by calling the class's explicit attention to the limitations of his or her perspective and encouraging a keen awareness of the third level of consciousness necessary to recognize this limitation. In this fashion Du Bois's double consciousness and the metaconsciousness it generates can be employed.

As a model for teaching, double consciousness directs attention to the interconnectedness of identity formation in the American racial landscape. We need to help our students decipher Bigger and the other characters in terms of the epistemological processes at work in *Native Son* and then turn the focus back on ourselves and on our students—looking first at the act of reading and then at the challenges to that reading and to the consciousnesses we posit. White teachers in particular need to articulate various perspectives to engage conventional discourses and epistemologies regarding race and the novel. The challenge is to avoid some form of white authentication and to avoid settling for a perpetuation of the double-consciousness formula in its simplest construction.

An approach to *Native Son* that emphasizes race and the epistemological constraints on understanding encourages attention to other concerns as well. Teachers will find it easy to situate Wright and *Native Son* in the history of African American letters and in what Gates identifies as the ideology of tradition and the "twin problematic of canon formation and nation formation" ("Studies" 294). Gates argues that "all definitions of ethnic tradition ultimately are both tautological and essentialist" and that "the process of constructing a group identity . . . involves active exclusion and repudiation" (293, 296). Wright's sensitivity to such issues is well known. His 1937 essay "Blueprint for Negro Writing" outlines a complex attitude toward a "nationalist spirit in Negro writing." Writing of "a nationalism whose reason for being lies in the simple fact of self-possession and in the consciousness of the interdependence of people in modern society," Wright calls attention to the racial and cultural components of identity (42). In turn, attention to the limitations of perspective and to the construction of identity and tradition will facilitate discussion of critical and pedagogical concerns in the academy that are mirrored in popular culture. *Native Son* speaks not to the legitimacy of white instruction of black texts or white direction of black films and plays but to the limitations inherent in such instruction and direction. One can recognize racial categories as cultural constructs and reject essentialism as Wright did and still have to confront those categories as real. Racial categories, once formed, whether culturally constructed and mutually constitutive or not, exist and assert their own subjectivities, just as Bigger does.

Gates writes of a "double vision," clearly descended from Du Bois's double consciousness, which is needed to investigate "how the [marginal] subjects are constructed or represented to themselves and . . . how they are represented within the cultural dominant" ("Studies" 299). Inverting the conventional perspective on the appropriation of ethnic material by white film directors, the black film director Bill Duke offers a concrete application of a perspective consonant with Gates's double vision and perfectly suited to the classroom.

> "Anybody can direct anything—but the point of view will be different. . . . I could direct a very decent Holocaust film," Duke says, "but I *don't* have the same experience as a young boy who was rocked to sleep in the lap of a grandmother who had a tattooed number on her arm, who told him stories of the people who disappeared, the relatives she never saw again, as he drifted off with his cheek nestled next to that number. It's those cultural nuances—and the ability to recognize and comprehend them—that make the difference."   (qtd. in Bates 38)

We would be wise to approach teaching *Native Son* with the same sensitivity to the strengths and weaknesses of our subjectivity.

A Missionary to "Her People" Teaches *Native Son*
Martha Satz

I teach at a medium-sized private university in Dallas, a school where most students are upper middle class and self-satisfied, respectful of their parents and their parents' values. The school sits in a "bubble," University Park, an incorporated city within Dallas that has its own school system and police and fire departments. Since virtually no African Americans or Hispanics live in this community, University Park police will routinely follow the car of an African American student until they verify that the driver attends the university. And students native to University Park report that the police's rule of thumb is that Hispanics without lawn mowers are suspicious. Two years ago, a well-known black director visiting in the prestigious theater department was arrested for "suspicious behavior"—jogging in University Park. Last year, when I asked students in a first-year honors seminar to write an essay about a moral dilemma in which they were involved, three young women wrote about their parents' discovering that they were dating black men. All the parents demanded that the young women immediately break off the relationship. Threats included refusing to finance the daughter's college education and disowning the daughter. We discussed the essays in class, and the students, with one exception, agreed that the women should obey their parents. Parents were parents, after all, and deserved respect. "Nothing could be as important as a parent's love," said one student.

I am disturbed by the environment at my school and by the responses of my students. My life experience differs radically from theirs. My ideals and the climate of the late sixties originally led me to Dallas from the Northeast to teach at a predominantly black institution, Bishop College, as part of a curriculum reform project sponsored by foundations and the federal government. During the six years I taught at Bishop and lived on campus, I learned a great deal about the complexity and pervasiveness of racism and about my own naïveté. My teaching experience was invaluable and profoundly rewarding, but I found it difficult always to be the object of suspicion—by students, colleagues, members of the community, and the politically radical consultants I encountered in the summer-long curriculum conferences. The consultants in particular were hostile to a group of which they took me to be a member: liberal white do-gooders coming to bring intellectual bounty from their benighted Ivy League background to "unfortunate black students." Angered and hurt by the consultants' response, I asked them what in their judgment a white academic concerned by the racial problems in the country could do. They answered, "Teach your own people about racial issues." At the time, I mentally dismissed their response, mostly because I didn't consider whites in general my people; but now, reflecting back on those words, I think that that may indeed be what I am engaged in.

I begin my account of teaching *Native Son* with this brief sketch of my students and myself, because I believe that reading texts, especially reading texts by black authors in our culture, acutely involves one's racial positioning in the society—that one's life experiences and the hue of one's skin greatly determine one's reading of most texts, and certainly a text as concerned with race as *Native Son*. My own racial locus as well as that of my students is part of the classroom interchange in our dealing with this novel. I agree with Michael Awkward's plea that white critics pay increased attention to what he calls self-referential acts when they interpret black texts. Awkward favorably cites Catharine Stimpson's account of her struggle as a white instructor teaching black texts. But Stimpson, discussing her course Books and the Black Experience, declares that she will not teach the course again: "White people at the moment have neither the intellectual skill nor the emotional clarity nor the moral authority to lead the pursuit of black studies" (2). I disagree. Although whites should not of course direct African American studies programs, I think it inevitable and actually valuable that they do teach black texts. If a white teacher foregrounds her racial positioning and encourages white students to do so as well, she then deals with the very issue of whites reading black texts. I confess that in my multiracial classroom I teach white students a good deal more than I do black students; in fact, I try to create an environment in which black students feel empowered to instruct white students. Black students, I hope, also benefit from studying the texts, for as Joyce Ann Joyce suggests, "the subtleties of . . . understanding [such texts] can lead to psychological freedom from the potentially enslaving white, hegemonic forces that attempt to subdue [black students]" ("Black Canon" 339).

In recent years I have taught *Native Son* in Minority Literature, a course that deals with African American, Hispanic, Asian American, Native American, and gay and lesbian literature in the American context. The course combines traditional literary exploration with an intense dialogue concerning students' beliefs about issues of race and oppression, issues raised by these texts. Because the class enjoys a certain word-of-mouth reputation, it characteristically has about thirty percent black students, a proportion that is quite unusual for the institution where I teach. Black students compose just four percent of the undergraduate student population, and most classes at the university have only one or two black students. However, many majority students enroll in my course not because of its reputation or appeal but simply because the course fulfills a requirement. So as the students enter the classroom the first day, they are often either visibly pleased or disconcerted by the composition of the class.

The first day, I talk about the obvious fact of the class's racial composition and reveal my ideological position. I make a speech something like this: "In most classes, we pretend that we are raceless and genderless, that we come to knowledge only as disembodied objective intellects. In this class, we will not make any such pretense. That we are white, that we are black, that we are male, that we are female will influence but not necessarily determine how we approach certain issues and certain literary texts. We will get angry with one another and even be tempted to call each other names like *racist*. Although we have been taught not to behave this way, especially in the classroom, I believe that on the whole such behavior may be productive. We are emotional and angry because these are important topics that involve all of us personally. We have been schooled not to discuss race, and that means that we know very little about the experiences and assumptions of one another. I also have strong opinions about race, and I will not pretend an objectivity that no one can have. You will know my opinions, and sometimes I will express them in a loud voice and with passion." At this point, I usually get a laugh, because some students, who have been in other classes of mine, know that I can get carried away in an argument. Some also know my son, who recently graduated from this school. Biracial (black and white), he was an officer in the Black Students Association and politically active in a number of arenas. Some students have also seen me walking around campus with my five-year-old biracial daughter in tow.

Many students look uncertain and skeptical about this speech. They seem not to know what to make of me or the course. We begin the semester not with literary texts but with theoretical works: Jean-Paul Sartre's *Anti-Semite and Jew*; Frantz Fanon's *Black Skin, White Masks*; "Primeval Mitosis," a chapter from Eldridge Cleaver's *Soul on Ice*. These works are supplemented with material on interracial sexuality and two videos by Marlon Riggs that explore racial stereotyping in media, *Ethnic Notions* and *Color Adjustment*. All this precedes *Native Son*, establishing not only a theoretical background for its reading but also a sense of the continuity of its content in the present moment. Thus *Native Son* culminates the class's month-long exploration, both academic and personal, of the psychological topography of prejudice. Our discussions of this work extend the evolving classroom dynamic already fraught with tension and punctuated by explosive, yet often illuminating, exchanges.

The class in its early stages is careful and polite. Sartre begins his discussion by saying that anti-Semitism, because it is directed against the being and rights of other persons, is not an "opinion" and should not be protected by the societal conventions that permit the expression of different views. I bring Sartre's position into the students' lives by inquiring about a concrete analogue. Should we, at a party, in the dorm, with our friends, at the family dinner table, tolerate racist remarks or jokes? How should we react to them? Students begin, almost universally, with a correct and sanctimonious response. They agree with Sartre. "Prejudiced views should not be tolerated under any circumstances," they say. Several white students give examples of how they chastise their friends and quote their own chilling responses to racist remarks. The African American students become increasingly restive and skeptical. "You mean you all always say something when you're out with your friends and somebody passes a remark?" they ask. I volunteer some of my own moments of social awkwardness or moral cowardice. Some white students then take a stab at honesty, talking about the difficulties of exchanges with their grandmothers and other elderly relatives. "You're supposed to respect your elders and not contradict them," they say. Conversation becomes increasingly frank as students talk about awkward social situations in which they are overwhelmed numerically or socially. "My father had his boss over . . ." Finally some protest, "Anyway, some jokes are funny, as long as no one you might offend is there." I ask about that, whether our response should be different if a member of the group who is the object of the humor is present. I refer to a joke my son had told me, "What is the first line of every nigger joke?" The answer and punchline—a gesture, the frantic craning of one's head to see if any of "them" are present.

Students by this time are eagerly coming to class to see whether there will be a confrontation. Sartre draws a harsh picture of the anti-Semite, pointing to his insecurity, his lack of reasoning, his desire to be anonymous. Sartre claims that a man (for Sartre the anti-Semite is always male) cannot be both an anti-Semite and, say, a good father and a good citizen, for such a man has chosen passion over reason, chosen to be governed by hatred. For Sartre, the anti-Semite who does not match this description is a mere echo, a nonperson, someone who assumes an anti-Semitic posture to fit in. Many white students find this portrayal overly harsh and general; they explicitly mention the racists in their families, beloved grandparents and aunts who are "very nice people." But Sartre's portrait of the anti-Semite is not nearly so controversial as his portrait of the democrat, the self-proclaimed friend of the Jew. The democrat's cardinal principle is that all people are the same, that being Jewish is as incidental a feature as having brown hair. Sartre condemns the democrat because the democrat robs Jews of their Jewishness. Many white students find this baffling; it contradicts conventional Sunday school pieties. We discuss the casual dismissal of differences occurring in ordinary conversational phrases like "My friend, who happens to be black." I venture a strong statement, presented as simply my own view, that blacks are importantly different from whites. I feel awkward saying this, fearful of being misunderstood by the African American students. Some in fact disagree, questioning expressions in their eyes. Others are prompted to talk about their differences—their culture and the sense of identity formed by a lifetime experience of oppression. They volunteer quotidian examples of racism: white students not getting on the elevator when they see a couple of black football players in it, black students being mistaken for janitorial staff, and so on. The disagreement, the diversity of views, and the fact that I have put myself at political risk with black students is, I think, instructive for white students. But many white students, their liberal platitudes having been punctured, want to know, "Well, what is the best way to deal with members of a minority?" By this time, they sound weary and frustrated. Some searching dialogue ensues.

Sartre's portrayal of the Jew, too, is interesting to students. For Sartre what defines Jews is that they are perceived as such by the community. Jews' response—authentic or inauthentic—to that perception is the important thing. In Sartre's view, inauthentic Jews internalize the negative stereotypes of themselves and act in a self-conscious effort to disassociate themselves from those stereotypes. Such people, for example, may talk in an excessively modulated voice and act with exaggerated generosity. I explain that Sartre's underlying existentialist assumptions emphasize the freedom of the individual. For Sartre, both the anti-Semite and the inauthentic Jew have chosen themselves, but both could have chosen otherwise.

We move on to Fanon's *Black Skin, White Masks*. Fanon writes in explicit dialogue with Sartre, altering and expanding Sartre's analysis to fit the black person in a colonial situation. He agrees with Sartre that Jews allow themselves to be poisoned by the stereotypes that others have of them, but he distinguishes the person of color from the Jew:

> The Jew is disliked from the moment he is tracked down. But in my case . . . I am the slave not of the "idea" that others have of me but of my own appearance. . . . I am being dissected under white eyes, the only real eyes. I am fixed. . . . I see in those white faces that it is not a new man who has come in, but a new kind of man, a new genus. Why, it's a Negro!
> (115–16)

In contrast to Sartre's Jew, Fanon's black experiences conceptual enslavement as a brutal fact, not as a choice. White colonial society imposes on the colonized a stereotype, language, system of values, and perceptual scheme, thereby forcing black people to regard themselves through the eyes of white people. Fanon graphically describes his own experience:

> I was responsible at the same time for my body, for my race, for my ancestors. . . . I was battered down by tom-toms, cannibalism, intellectual deficiency, fetishism, racial defects, slave-ships and above all else, above all: "Sho' good eatin'."
> (112)

Fanon's concept, which he terms third-person consciousness, the minority person's regarding himself through the white person's eyes, becomes a key notion in our classroom. Apparently, Fanon has identified something vital for African American students. They inevitably cite third-person consciousness as the most significant idea of the semester when they evaluate the course. Fanon's phrase becomes the term to explain their own experiences—sitting in a classroom, walking across the campus.

The majority students, however, are resistant to the notion. "I see everybody as the same," they say. "Why should they be feeling different?" I tell a story that sometimes helps. In the first years of teaching this course, when the student population was almost completely white, Nikki Giovanni came to give a reading during Black Emphasis Month. I offered students extra credit to attend the performance and write a review. They returned to class the next day, disturbed by their experience. "Everybody there was black, and people looked at us strangely, as if they wanted to know why we were there. And Nikki Giovanni just assumed that everyone she was talking to was black." I point out to my class that for these students the experience was novel and short but offered an inkling of what life is like every day for minority people in this country.

I then show *Ethnic Notions* to make Fanon's concept of third-person consciousness graphic and familiar. The video presents the pervasive caricature of blacks in American culture in artifacts, the printed media, movies, and cartoons. The images in Bugs Bunny cartoons, greeting cards, and household items such as brand-name products, ashtrays, and doorstops particularly strike the students. The video traces certain stereotypes in media—the Sambo, the Zip Coon, the Black Brute, the Mammy, and the Pickaninny—and shows how these images work ideologically to support the white power structure. For example, on the video Barbara Christian discusses how the desexualized, nurturing Mammy serves to repress the threat the black female slave presents to the slave's mistress. Black students leave the classroom saddened by the pervasiveness of these vulgar, demeaning images. Some white students seem to experience small epiphanies, looking about themselves with new eyes, seeing for the first time offensive images in children's books, in ads, and on their neighbors' lawns. The video also creates a new tension in the classroom: if white students should laugh at a pratfall in a racist cartoon or at grinning black children eating watermelon, they are immediately silenced by looks of loathing.

I follow *Ethnic Notions* by projecting the cover of the 1988–89 Dallas telephone book on the wall. The illustration depicts three children, black, white, and Hispanic, using different telephone devices. A white girl with an intelligent look, clad in neat school clothes, converses on a standard telephone. A Hispanic girl, conservatively dressed, soberly uses a computer device. And a grinning black boy, sporting a baseball cap and a football jersey, happily puts a toy can to his ear. The discussion that ensues is always incendiary. African American students, having just viewed forty years of denigrating images, shake their heads and say, "Same old, same old, another grinning black boy who can run and play sports but is too ignorant to know that he doesn't have a real telephone." Some white students audibly gasp when the image appears before them. Many from the area had seen the phone book cover before but had never seen "how horrible it was." "How could something so bad be on the telephone directory?" they ask.

But a strong contingent of white students argue vigorously that there is nothing wrong. The boy is dressed like a boy. How should he dress, in a coat and tie? He's playing with a toy phone because that's what kids do. It's the girls in fact who are distorted; children of that age are not so serious. Would anyone complain if the white girl had the toy phone? Anyone who finds this cover offensive, they argue, is just looking for a reason to be offended. They are adamant, resentful, secure in their position. They pass remarks to one another under their breath.

The question arises: Do we think that the artist was intentionally trying to be racist? I take this opportunity to discuss the self-perpetuation of racist stereotypes. Artists, I venture, in drawing their images, unconsciously summon all the other images of black boys they have seen. They do not invent the stereotype; they continue it. How, I ask, was this image allowed in every household in Dallas? Surely, the telephone company did not want to alienate its clientele. The black students say that obviously there are not blacks on the review board. I ask whether whites as well shouldn't see the racism in this image. "Well, now, after seeing this movie, I would," one young white woman responds. Some of us nod in appreciation.

African American students, galvanized by the polarized positions in this discussion, make plans to disrupt the seating arrangements of the classroom. A certain, rather belligerent, group of white students sit in a bloc and habitually make remarks under their breath. The black students plan to sit among them, not allowing them to do this. They are going to change them, or at least change their behavior.

Showing *Color Adjustment* softens the mood of the classroom and blurs the sharply drawn lines. The video traces the portrayal of blacks in television from 1948 to 1988 up to the *Cosby Show*. All the students enjoy watching the old TV clips; all recognize the unflattering portraits in shows such as *Amos and Andy* and *Beulah*, and all are somewhat puzzled by the video's gibes against "positive images" in shows such as the 1960s *Julia*, the 1970s *Roots*, and the more recent *Cosby Show*.

The loud and contentious atmosphere of the class abruptly shifts to hushed silence when I introduce the topic of interracial sexuality. I mention the incidents of Emmett Till and Yusef Hawkins and the fact that castration was a part of most lynchings. I quote the old southern white cliché of the 1950s: "They can go to school with us and eat in the same restaurants, but would you want your sister to marry one?" I ask the students, Why is sex the last bastion of racism? Students have looks of both discomfort and recognition. Is it really racist, some ask, to want to stay in your own group? The children of interracial relationships really have a hard time. I mention a remark of Spike Lee quoted in the *New York Times*: "There's something about black men being with white women that threatens white men. And that's why Yusef Hawkins was killed" (Freedman 22).

We go on to read "Primeval Mitosis," even though I agree with Stimpson that Cleaver is "bombastic, schematic, vicious to homosexuals, unfair to white women" (1). Employing the structure of myth, Cleaver provocatively elucidates a theory expressed by other, perhaps more sophisticated writers. He describes a primeval rift, one imposed not by the gods but by society. In his view, unitary man has been divided into body and mind, the beast and the administrator, the supermasculine menial and the omnipotent administrator. Cleaver does not refer to race, but color leaps out from every sentence. I try to make his ideas palpable for my class. Why is American society in general content to acknowledge the superior physical skills of blacks? Norman Podhoretz epitomizes the attitude in a remark quoted as an epigraph to the essay that follows "Primeval Mitosis":

> . . . just as in childhood I envied Negroes for what seemed to me their superior masculinity, so I envy them today for what seems to me their

> superior physical grace and beauty. . . . I am now capable of aching with all my being when I watch a Negro couple on the dance floor, or a Negro playing baseball or basketball. They are on the kind of terms with their own bodies that I should like to be on with mine, and for that precious quality they seem blessed to me.   (Cleaver, "Convalescence" 191)

We talk about Podhoretz's posture in this remark. I ask why sports fans, even racist ones, feel a strong identification with black players who play on "their team." I talk about how sports teams have traditional black positions and white positions. Students, more versed than I in sports lore, supply additional information; they also cite the lack of black managers. Last semester, a black football player wistfully told how his school counselor discussed with him his potential opportunities in football despite the young man's extraordinary academic achievement test scores.

After this discussion, students seem to recognize the validity of Cleaver's categories. Cleaver employs the division to discuss, rather startlingly, the white man's envy for the black man:

> Fearing impotence, impotence being implicit in his negation and abdication of his Body, his profoundest need is for evidence of his virility. . . . [t]he Omnipotent Administrator cannot help but covertly . . . envy the bodies and strength of the most alienated men beneath him. . . .
> (182)

In this light, we talk about the common myth of the black man's exaggerated penis size. Almost all the males visibly react to this discussion, black males grinning and strutting just a bit, white males looking uncomfortable and resentful. But I remind them of the mythological tradeoff: genitalia grow and brains shrink. Cleaver emphasizes that the taboo against sexual involvement between the black man and the white woman exists because of the white man's insecurity, his envy of the black man, and the desire of the white woman for the black man. Students corroborate many of Cleaver's contentions by reference to Spike Lee's *Jungle Fever*.

Cleaver subordinates women to men. The white woman's image enhances her man's: "[S]he seeks to increase the weakness of her body and stamp out all traces of strength, to differentiate it further from the effeminate form of her man" (183). For Cleaver, the major concern and fear of the white woman is frigidity.

He subordinates black women to all the other characters in his analysis. In the classroom, I use the corrective voice of Michelle Wallace to express the stereotype of the black woman:

> [The image] is of a woman of inordinate strength, with an ability for tolerating an unusual amount of misery and heavy, distasteful work. This

woman does not have the same fears, weaknesses, and insecurities as other women, but believes herself to be and is, in fact, stronger emotionally than most men. Less of a woman in that she is less "feminine" and helpless, she is really more of a woman in that she is the embodiment of Mother Earth, the quintessential mother with infinite sexual life-giving and nurturing reserves. In other words, she is a superwoman.   (107)

Although Cleaver discusses the sexual attraction between white man and black woman, he makes it secondary to the other interracial pairing. To supplement Cleaver's discussion, we therefore read selections from Deborah Gray White's *Ar'n't I a Woman*, which details the victimization, rape, and suffering of women slaves, who were as a matter of course the sexual property of their masters and the despised but unacknowledged rivals of their mistresses. We also expand the portrait of the white woman beyond that of a person obsessed by fears of frigidity. Lillian Smith's remark in *Killers of the Dream* reveals the complexity of the white woman's position: "To perpetuate the idea of her ice-like purity, the Southern white woman had to give up, at least in principle and often in fact, the two major erotic joys of a woman's life: the passion of her husband's desire, and the nursing of her infants" (87). Personal questions arise from this material. Last semester, a young black woman asked me why black women were considered promiscuous, when she and none of her friends in fact were. For the first time, white students look around at the color spectrum of so-called black people in this country and understand the wholesale rape that must have taken place. Students come to understand that the issue of interracial sexuality is more complex than they had at first thought.

Thus the class begins its study of *Native Son* with a sophisticated conceptual apparatus, experience of confrontation with personal prejudice, and a knowledge of the pervasiveness of racist assumptions in American culture. Sartre has provided the students with an explanation of the dynamics of prejudice and with portraits of the bigot and the liberal. He has provided the categories of authentic and inauthentic to characterize the response of those who are the objects of prejudice. Fanon has supplied an analysis of the colonial situation, the unique situation of the person of color, and the inevitability of third-person consciousness. Cleaver has given deep cultural and psychological explanations for the taboo against interracial sexuality. And *Ethnic Notions* and *Color Adjustment* have detailed the stereotypes of blacks in our historical tradition, the ideological function of such stereotypes, and their persistence in contemporary culture.

Native Son always enthralls and excites students; when the curriculum described above precedes its reading, the pleasures of familiarity and recognition are added. As we open our discussion of the novel, we are reminded of racial differences in the classroom. I ask the students why the protagonist is named Bigger. Black students respond immediately—because it sounds like *nigger*. White students typically react as if this sound similarity is a revelation to them. After students offer other answers, I furnish a rather literary response: Although

Bigger is like many other blacks, his drama is played out on a grander stage.

The opening scene provides fertile territory to begin discussion. We focus on the image of Bigger's family looking away in shame. Beyond the literal circumstances of not wishing to see one another's nakedness, the shame resonates in other ways. I read a brief passage of explication:

> He hated his family because he knew that they were suffering and that he was powerless to help them. He knew that the moment he allowed himself to feel to its fullness how they lived, the shame and misery of their lives, he would be swept out of himself with fear and despair. . . . He knew that the moment he allowed what his life meant to enter fully into his consciousness, he would either kill himself or someone else.   (9)

I remark that Bigger lives in a completely separate black environment, where every aspect of his life and thought gives evidence of the superiority of whiteness and the corresponding inferiority of blackness. I mention examples of the two divided worlds: Bigger and his friends' playing white, emulating a barely imagined way of life (18–20), and the famous airplane passage where Bigger contemplates all the barriers that separate him from his goal of flying a plane (16–17). Students provide more examples: Bigger and his friends' being afraid to rob a white store although they have robbed black stores countless times, and *Trader Horn*, the black movie Bigger and Jack attend, with "pictures of naked black men and women whirling in dances and . . . drums beating" (36). The student referring to this passage mentions *Ethnic Notions*; she understands the kind of movie Bigger and Jack are watching.

I develop the thesis that Bigger tries, however unsuccessfully, to shut out his feelings of inferiority as long as he is in a black environment but that when he enters the white world, such repression is impossible. We hark back to what Fanon says: "As long as the black man is among his own, he will have no occasion, except in minor internal conflicts, to experience his being through others" (109). But, as Fanon puts it, "then the occasion arose when I had to meet the white man's eyes" (110). Of course Bigger in Chicago's South Side is not among his own; he is in a colonial world, a world created by a white power structure. But when he moves into the white world, he becomes more acutely aware of himself through others' eyes. As he approaches the Dalton house, he muses:

> Would they expect him to come in the front way or back? . . . Suppose a policeman saw him wandering in a white neighborhood like this? It would be thought that he was trying to rob or rape somebody. . . . Why had he come to take this goddamn job? He could have stayed among his own people and escaped feeling this fear and hate.   (49)

Fanon, developing his notion of third-person consciousness, remarks: "In the white world the man of color encounters difficulties in the development of his bodily scheme. Consciousness of the body is solely a negating activity" (109). Bigger in the Dalton household, sinking into a chair, "found a tall, lean, white-haired man holding a piece of paper in his hand. The man was gazing at him with an amused smile that made him conscious of every square inch of skin on his black body" (52). In such scenes students recognize third-person consciousness in its most intense form.

Taking a cue from this sequence of images, we discuss the prominence and omnipresence of the white gaze in the first part of the book, a gaze projected even by the Daltons' white cat. Students themselves realize the symmetry between the white cat in the Dalton household and the black rat in the Thomas household, enjoying the relation. They also note with horror that Mary continues to stare at Bigger even after death. This insight gives them a sense of Bigger's fate.

Mary is an intriguing and controversial character for the students, and they split radically in interpreting her, but not along predictable racial lines. Recently in a class, one white student said that Mary deserved what she got, but a black student said that Mary is better than all the others in her environment because, unlike them, she is trying to bridge racial barriers, however ineptly.

Students recognize something of themselves in Mary. They interpret her as rebelling against her parents. Her defiance of her family explains why she disrupts Bigger's interview with her father, asking Bigger about his union participation. But despite their identification with her, students get angry with Mary for her selfishness. She is continually embarrassing Bigger, seems to try to get him fired before he is even hired, and tacitly encourages her boyfriend, Jan, to shake his hand even though it is mortifying to Bigger: "[T]hey made him feel his black skin by just standing there looking at him, one holding his hand and the other smiling" (76). The students link Mary to Sartre's democrat, although they find differences as well. Mary never sees Bigger or appreciates his feelings or desires; her principles blind her to Bigger's individuality. We discuss whether Mary is a racist, particularly in the passage when she tries to befriend Bigger (in the following passage, all the ellipses except the first are in the original text):

> "You know, Bigger, I've long wanted to go into those houses . . . and just *see* how your people live. You know what I mean? I've been to England, France and Mexico, but I don't know how people live ten blocks from me. We know so *little* about each other. I just want to *see.* I want to *know* these people. Never in my life have I been inside of a Negro home. Yet they *must* live like we live. They're *human*. . . . There are twelve million of them. . . . They live in our country. . . . In the same city with us. . . ." her voice trailed off wistfully.
> (79)

This passage enrages most black students. They focus on its condescension. "She sounds as if she wants to take a field trip, like going to the zoo," one student comments. Another says, "It reminds me of my roommate wanting to feel my hair." I volunteer a story as well. When my son was young, a woman wanted him to come play with her son because "it would be good for her son to play with a black child." But both white and black students condemn the violent attack on Mary. They say: "She's trying; she's trying. In that time and place she's doing the best she can. She wants to understand. Sure, she's doing it in a condescending manner, but she's doing the best she can. What can she do?" Some of the students talking this way seem to be giving voice to their own frustrations rather than simply defending Mary. Given all they have heard so far in this class, what can they do?

Some students, black students, have a further theory about Mary: she is attracted to Bigger. Why else does she drink with him, go to his part of town, and sit in the front seat with him? Some students seem taken aback by this view. But all of us are now self-conscious about how we interpret interracial relationships.

As a classroom exercise, I ask students to write down where in book 1 ("Fear") Bigger has made a mistake. He ends up killing a woman, putting her body in the furnace, and chopping off her head. Where in the chain of actions leading to this did he go wrong? Independently thinking about my question, students produce an interesting range of responses. One student suggests that Bigger never should have taken the job in the Dalton house. He took it with the wrong motive. The white movie suggested that he might get involved with the young woman of the household. The student is hooted down. The students generally believe that Bigger needed to take the job to keep his family from starvation. Some say that Bigger should have refused to drive Mary to her secret meeting with Jan; he should have informed her father of her intentions. Most students reject this response too. Bigger would have lost his job; Mary would have made up a story about him. One thoughtful young black man says that Bigger should not have drunk liquor with Jan and Mary, for this act crossed the employee-employer barrier. His classmates disagree, saying that Bigger was pressured to drink; he was trying to please his bosses. Most students believe that Bigger's practical mistake was taking Mary upstairs to her room; his moral error was molesting her as she lay there unconscious. But there are disagreements here as well. It was kindness and consideration that led him to take Mary upstairs. "No," say a contingent of young black men. "A black man does not go into a white woman's bedroom, period. No no no." Somewhat surprisingly, a group of young women students defend Bigger's touching Mary: "Any man would do the same, especially when the woman is forbidden fruit," they remark, revealing perhaps a rather low regard of men in general. Several white students identify Bigger's mistake in attempting to cover his tracks once he discovers the killing. He is innocent; he should just explain how it all happened. This answer is roundly rejected. As one young black man put it, "He did what every brother would and should do in those circumstances." At the end of this discussion, most students agree that Bigger made no grave errors, that every step he took was understandable, that he committed no grave moral errors.

Students' view of Bigger's moral culpability in book 2 radically shifts because of his affirmation of the killing and his brutal murder of Bessie, more the former than the latter. Most students, like Mr. Max in the last book of the novel, cannot understand Bigger's embracing of his deed, but some—more black students than white—do try hesitatingly to explain their perception of Bigger to their classmates. Using Sartre's notion, they say that Bigger has become authentic. Rather than flee from the stereotype of the murderous, raping black brute, he embraces it, becomes it, and tries to transform it. He is not stupid, but he is in a murderous rage—and for good reason. Most students listen to this explanation with difficulty. It is very difficult material to take in.

In response to my questions, the students focus on why Bigger often risks his life to buy a newspaper. Material from Fanon, Sartre, and the videos come together in this discussion. Students are not shocked by the press's portrayal of Bigger, because they know the history and pervasiveness of such portrayals. They have seen remnants of it even in their city's recent phone book cover. Attributing to Bigger some intuitive understanding of Sartre and Fanon, they appreciate why the imagery in which his story is told is so important. Thus they understand why he feels so powerful when he gets to tell the story. They examine the interplay of imagery in the latter part of the book: the way the black workers discuss Bigger's crime and how the white perception of it affects them; how all the book's black characters stand as one in a jail cell, with the white gaze on them.

There is general sadness about the role of Bessie in the novel. She is seen, especially by black women, as the symbol of the eternally victimized black woman. She is victimized by Bigger. She is victimized by society: her body, even in death, does the work of the white woman. Her life and death stand for nothing—in Bigger's eyes, in the white society's eyes, and even perhaps in the narrator's eyes.

I ask students whether by the end of the novel Wright holds out any hope of a relationship between the races. There is fierce debate about the motives and moral worth of Mr. Max. "He never really understands Bigger," say many of the black students. "He's trying. He's giving him a voice in the white community," rejoin many of the white students. This is the most I can expect from the discussion.

Native Son and Its Readers

Robert Felgar

For most of the twenty years I have been teaching *Native Son*, I have taught it the way I was taught: I have pointed out various patterns of imagery, discussed moral responsibility and racism, analyzed point of view, argued whether or not the protagonist is redeemed in some sense at the end of the novel, debated whether or not Wright endorses Max's speech to the judge, cited the novel's literary antecedents and successors, and so forth. The classroom results for my students and for me became deadly: I was telling them, I was doing the reading for them. A challenging and exciting novel was in danger of becoming a corpse for me and for my students, and we were nearing the postmortem. I do not at all mean that the questions mentioned above do not come up anymore or that teachers who use the lecture approach for *Native Son* are wrong; I mean only that lecturing about such matters was no longer effective in my classes. In the mid-1980s I did a pedagogical about-face: I combined reader-response criticism and cultural criticism to see if I could transform my traditional classroom from a morgue into a site of lively and productive debate and discussion. The classroom results from using this two-pronged approach to teaching *Native Son* have been very encouraging.

The approach works because it foregrounds what literary study is all about: the personal experience of reading. Personal experience is far more interesting to most students than are generalizations about assigned texts. Getting students intellectually involved with their responses to *Native Son* stimulates them much more than abstract statements will. If teachers perform the work (that is, read carefully) for them, many students will have little incentive to do it for themselves, and in their reading they will be aware largely of what the teachers emphasized, not of aspects of the text that might have spontaneously roused their own interest.

If reader-response criticism enables the evocation of students' experiences of *Native Son*, cultural criticism provides a way of explaining why students have different experiences with this novel (or with any other literary work). The emphasis is on the students: students experience *Native Son* and account for that experience rather than simply memorize the teacher's or the literary critic's transactions with the novel. Reader-response criticism alone is valuable but often fails to account for students' literary experience. The combination of the two critical stances deals not only with the responses of particular readers but also with the cultural and ideological causes of those responses.

Most students will need some exposition of the two theories on which my approach is based, but I do not provide it until after they have read *Native Son*. Cultural criticism is a strategy that pries out hidden, excluded, or repressed ideological assumptions, the concealed sources of authority, buried cultural work. Two good examples of cultural criticism are Ellen Rooney's *Seductive Reasoning: Pluralism as the Problematic of Contemporary Literary Theory* and

Mary Poovey's *Uneven Developments: The Ideological Work of Gender in Mid-Victorian England*. Rooney shows how pluralistic literary theory, by denying it is a theory, can appropriate, through its discourse, nonpluralistic literary theory. Pluralism, acting as if it is "natural," thus hides the source of its power. Poovey makes the same point about gender in Victorian literature. In *David Copperfield*, for instance, Charles Dickens acts as if the categories "man" and "woman" are completely natural rather than constructed; the novel's cultural and social power can be demystified once the reader sees that Dickens has hidden the source of that power. Of the many competing varieties of reader-response theory, I prefer Louise M. Rosenblatt's, as set forth in her *Literature as Exploration* and *The Reader, the Text, the Poem*, because she maintains a balance between the claims of the reader and those of the text. She sees literary reading as a transaction between reader and text, each shaping and constraining the other, each producing the other. Rather than reduce the text to a mere opportunity for bricolage or psychoanalysis, her responsible reader acknowledges the constraints of the text without being imprisoned by them.

To illustrate how reader-response criticism and cultural criticism can be explained to students, who are not always comfortable with theory, I first mention some examples taken from life instead of from a literary text. I often begin consideration of *Native Son* by posing two questions to the class: When did you realize you were black or white? And what would your reaction be if you asked for flesh-colored bandages in a drugstore and were given dark rather than pink ones? Invariably, white students (the enrollment at Jacksonville State University, where I teach, is eighteen percent black, eighty-two percent white, although in an African American literature survey the class is likely to be half black or more) cannot answer the first question, but all black students remember all too well when they first learned their place in America's racial lineup. In answer to my first question, one black student told the class that he and his brother, both light-skinned, were playing in their yard once when a white child asked him, "What race are you?" He answered, "I don't know; I guess we're niggers." My first question makes students aware of, and challenges, what many of them automatically assume, that being white is the norm, the privileged category. If you have any doubts about whether you are in that category, you are in racial trouble in this country. Cultural criticism of the notion of race can make students realize that the idea that it goes without saying that white is the standard should not go without saying. In answer to my second question, many white students will reveal their surprise, dismay in some cases, that flesh-colored bandages might be designed for dark skin. Encouraging students to ferret out the reasons for their responses to my two questions makes ideological assumptions available for analysis. White students can come to understand that their sense of racial superiority is based on untenable premises. This same strategy—carefully and honestly monitoring and accounting for response—I apply to *Native Son*, with classroom results that are often intriguing. Success in the classroom is largely a result of oral discussion, although as I explain later, I use other methods too. Depending on how lively a class is and on how student-centered a teacher wants the class to be, the teacher can play a lesser or greater role in the discussion of responses and their causes. In other words, how often the teacher intervenes will be determined by how much autonomy the students have.

If I have a lively class, I can apply my approach with relative ease—students take the book and run with it once they see how. But regardless of the kind of class I have, I tell several students that they will be responsible for stimulating class discussion, using my approach. Of course, I am always ready to provide friendly coaching and nudging if student-led discussion breaks down or moves toward a dead end. Since students know they will eventually all have a chance to lead discussion (even if not on *Native Son*), they are sympathetic to the plights of nervous discussion leaders. Consider a discussion of the scene in which Bigger smothers Mary. It is one of the most culturally, socially, politically, and sexually charged episodes in American literature. Students who will admit how threatening it is can come to terms with the irrational basis of their fear by asking one another why a black man's presence in a white woman's bedroom is so upsetting. Discussion of the scene, and of its ending in death rather than in lovemaking, can fill an entire class period. Students begin thinking hard about what their reactions reveal of American culture, about why in some lynchings of black men the victims were also castrated, about what Shakespeare was up to in the scene in *Othello* where Othello kills Desdemona, about what Mary might represent to Bigger and Bigger to Mary. These issues and others readily emerge in a candid, student-led discussion. And a class can come to understand that a culture's values are not given but negotiable.

My classroom experience indicates that although teachers will agree with Rosenblatt that every reading experience is different from every other (I would also suggest that there are transparadigmatic elements in different student readers), some major categories of responses can be productively analyzed and dealt with. The "generic" white readers in my classes tend to bring certain racial assumptions to *Native Son* that Nathan Irvin Huggins has elucidated in *Harlem Renaissance*. Huggins posits a white Puritan culture that officially endorses such values as hard work, responsibility, sexual continence, honesty, formal education. Finding it impossible to embody these values consistently, the members of this group, Huggins maintains, vicariously satisfy the need for release from them by inventing another culture that is lazy, irresponsible, incontinent, dishonest, lacking in formal education. Many white readers of *Native Son* will find in Bigger proof that the stereotype Huggins dismantles is true, because they will not realize that Wright is challenging them by seeming to confirm their expectation of what black men are like. Unaware of Wright's maneuver, such readers are often unwilling to forgo their sense of white superiority because they have so much psychological and emotional energy invested in it. To accept that Bigger, although in some sense a native son of America, an example of its racial structure, is as human as they are would disrupt their (often unstated and unrecognized) belief in that superiority. If such readers sense that race is an unprincipled source of social authority, they often lack the social confidence to part with that authority; in their eyes, the price is too high. When Wright confronts them with Bigger Thomas, a literalization of their racial expectations, yet at the same time holds them partly accountable for Bigger's existence, many of them feel threatened and become angry. My approach to *Native Son* shows students that Wright took a bold gamble in providing such readers with just what their racist perspective causes them to see: the black male as homicidal maniac. These readers have to be encouraged to look more closely at why Bigger is the way he is.

Perhaps the worst nightmare a teacher using my approach to *Native Son* can have is the extreme (but fortunately rare) version of the generic white reader: the testosterone-poisoned, hypermasculine white male reader. A product of seeing too many *Dirty Harry* and *Terminator* films, this student is so threatened by Bigger Thomas that he may storm out—he has stormed out—of the classroom. When it happened, the effect on the remaining students was interesting: most of the black students were amused, but the white students seemed embarrassed. I let his departure pass but talked to him privately later on, whereupon he calmed down and continued to come to (and stayed in) class. Such adrenaline-induced reactions are not easy to deal with, although they do demonstrate the unusually strong challenge *Native Son* presents to its audience. One teaching strategy is to use cultural criticism in private office consultations to encourage such angry readers to take a dispassionate look at their anger and its causes. But they may feel they have too much to lose, as members of a social hierarchy based on race and patriarchy, to rethink their behavior.

In contrast, some black male readers in my classes are deeply torn in their responses to *Native Son*. They acknowledge that when Bigger tells Bessie whites "done killed plenty of us" and she replies, "That don't make it [killing Mary] right" (204), her position is irrefutable, but they are also unwilling to see Bigger's killing of Mary as just an accident, as some readers argue. Young black male readers know, too well, that attributing the first murder to uncontrollable fear of whites makes Bigger's horrifying killing and decapitation of Mary an act devoid of significance. No matter how reprehensible that act is, these readers claim value for it as an expression of defiance against white racism. The hidden ideological assumption here, as cultural criticism can reveal, is that Bigger had no way to resist the white world except through violence. Asking such readers if that assumption should be dismantled is not easy, but it can be done through persistent coaching by the teacher and other students.

Teaching *Native Son* to women with this approach can generate particularly lively discussions. As sympathetic as they may be to Bigger as a member of an oppressed group, they are of course extremely angry at his treatment of Vera Thomas, Mrs. Thomas, Mary Dalton, and Bessie Mears. Taught to use my two-pronged approach, women readers of *Native Son* undo Wright's gender-based premises. They also learn better than to be daunted by the observation that women read too personally when they take "mere textual constructions" like Mary and Bessie to be mimetic. Of the many treatments of Wright's often debated misogyny in *Native Son*, teachers may want to cite Trudier Harris's argument that "black women . . . are portrayed as being in league with the oppressors of black men" (63). Harris adds social class to gender when she remarks that Wright is suggesting (in the scene where Bigger's family visits him after his arrest) that "a large part of Bigger's problem is that he is descended from such an ignorant, praying group of backward 'niggers'" (69). Harris's observations have a lot to do with the intense and understandable anger some women, especially African American women, express in their heated reactions to *Native Son*. Although I am a middle-aged white male teacher, I know that examining this area of readers' response can make students, particularly black students, quite uncomfortable. Doing it is risky, and trust is crucial. The venturesome teacher can use the feminist issue as a springboard to interesting questions for the classroom: What is the significance of Bigger's killing two women and not two men? Are black women holding him down, and if they are, does this have anything to do with white male power? Is Mrs. Thomas merely trying to prepare her older son for what she knows he must face? Does Wright himself think that the smothering of Mary Dalton is worse than the smashing of Bessie's head in with a brick? Where and how did Bigger acquire his attitude toward women, especially black women? Mentioning the strategic omission of Bessie's murder in the 1986 film version of the novel can lead to revealing discussions of the relationship between Bigger and Bessie in the novel. Women in my classes tend to respond to *Native Son* not as men do: that difference can dramatize Wright's own dubious response toward black women.

More and more, I find that students' responses of any type are shaped by the popular media. Teachers should ask themselves and their students to what extent their reactions to Bigger and to Wright's treatment of race and gender are a product of contemporary films, television (consider the Willie Horton ads), newspapers, and magazines. Bigger himself looks in the newspaper for confirmation of his first killing. I encourage student readers to ask themselves how much of their response to Bigger is based on expectations about black men acquired from watching, often uncritically, *New Jack City* or *Do the Right Thing*, for example. Their response to Bigger may be determined by how he compares with the young black men played by Wesley Snipes and Spike Lee, respectively, in those films. In my experience, our students are no more aware of how much popular culture has determined the way they read than Bigger is of how much his view of himself is based on the films, newspapers, and magazines that produced him.

I should cite one major caveat for teachers who want to use cultural criticism and reader-response criticism to teach *Native Son*. Our students own and operate very sensitive classroom radar, which quickly registers the normative signals teachers emit in class. If these signals are suspected of indicating which readers' responses are connected to high grades, then there will be no candid, spontaneous revelation of responses. I have tried several tactics, with varying degrees of success, to jam this radar. I ask students to draw or sketch different scenes in *Native Son*, scenes chosen by them or by me—the decapitation of Mary, Bigger in Mary's bedroom, Bigger smashing Bessie's head in with a brick, Bigger torturing Gus, Bigger in a room with most of the other characters, and so on. Such drawings reveal a wide range of responses, because no one can know beforehand which drawing, if any, will have the highest market (i.e., classroom) value. Everyone gets the chance to see everyone else's. The most admired drawing is usually the one that results in the most interesting discussion. If teachers overcome their feeling that the assignment is "highschoolish," these drawings can suggest a good deal about the illustrators and about what is being illustrated. One student made Bigger twice Mary's size in the scene where Bigger decapitates Mary—a disregard for representational art that has interesting ideological implications. These visual interpretations of *Native Son* are then interpreted by the students, with unexpected and often humorous results. Invariably, someone will ask if a drawing is faithful to Wright's text. I think it provocative that Wright does not describe Bigger's face, although the *Tribune* provides the ideologically inflected report that Bigger's "lower jaw protrudes obnoxiously, reminding one of a jungle beast" (322). Most students will turn to the appropriate passages to see if they conflict in any way with the pictures, so the text constrains visual representation. Often students ask one another why they drew Bessie or some other character a certain way, but if they do not, the teacher can raise the issue.

Parody and satire provide another way to jam classroom radar. Suggesting a parodic rewriting of Buckley's speech to the judge or a satirical revision of the bedroom scene can disrupt unchallenged assumptions about the novel.

Having students write Bessie's letter to Bigger (in the book we know only that she tells him she will not participate in the ransom scheme [352]) is also a tactic that helps students resist the authority of the instructor and the novel. If these student letters are unsigned, the anonymity may help ensure spontaneous responses to the book. With a novel as disturbing as *Native Son*, some readers will be guarded no matter how much trust there is in the classroom. Black and white students are often so leery of what to say in front of one another that some teachers may want to assure such students that no one but the teacher will read their responses. (Sometimes these students eventually begin to feel confident enough to describe their reading experience to the class, but not always.)

The key point is that students need to respond before their responses are shaped or edited by classroom pressures. Students need the opportunity to challenge or resist the teacher's (often unstated) ideological authority, but few will challenge or resist openly if they are worried about the effect on their grade. Open discussions of *Native Son* based on my approach will, I acknowledge, produce off-the-wall interpretations—one of my students admitted she particularly hated Bigger for incinerating Mary, because cremation precluded bodily resurrection—but where the wall is becomes negotiable, which is exactly as it should be. Unless students feel free to express their responses, whether anonymously or publicly, we will never know what those responses were and never have the chance to examine them.

One response to *Native Son* that I have been trying to elicit in students is awareness of Wright's quiet undoing of allochronic discourse (discourse that denies coevalness) and its ideological underpinnings. In *Time and the Other*, Johannes Fabian convincingly demonstrates how the West has denied the rest of the world coevalness. Fabian argues that the West, by insisting on its distance in time from the non-West, has kept non-Western societies, particularly Asian and African societies, inferior to it. The consequent "primitiveness" or "savagery" of cultures supposedly remote in time has served as a justification of Western imperialism. I ask students to note that when Bigger sees *Trader Horn* (a popular film of the 1930s), he senses only vaguely, if at all, the quiet but devastating cultural damage being done by a film that puts black Africans, Bigger's ancestors, in a remote time and place, à la *Heart of Darkness*. The class can then resist the cultural manipulation the film performs on Bigger. It is this same temporal remoteness that Buckley, the state's attorney, cites as a reason Bigger should be executed: otherwise, Buckley argues, society will revert to a prelaw state. Allochronicity is so deeply buried in our students' cultural consciousness, as well as in our own, that a class will never resist the ideological influence the device exerts if the instructor does not nudge student readers in that direction.

I have hardly exhausted readers' responses to the issues of race, gender, and time in *Native Son*. There are many other elements in the novel students react to—the setting, politics, religion, conclusion, to name a few. Nor do I mean to suggest there is a master reader or master discourse that can completely and permanently appropriate *Native Son* or that *Native Son* (or any other novel) is a master narrative. What I do want to suggest is that our culture is generating readers who, for many ideological reasons, are producing many different versions of *Native Son* (and of any other text we read). Teachers and students can teach one another that Wright's novel, like any other cultural artifact, is going to be the product of a dynamic interplay between exegesis and eisegesis (interpretation that expresses the interpreter's own ideas and biases). Where readers are situated (racially, socially, culturally) enables and constrains what they see, or do not see, in *Native Son*. This problem is troubling, students come to understand, because even if they inspect the intellectual lenses they are looking through, they can do so only through another pair of intellectual lenses.

My approach to *Native Son* is most useful in that it makes often passive students actively aware of their racial, gender-based, social, cultural, and allochronic assumptions and explains to them why, in *Black Boy*, the usually rational and implacably secular young Wright was willing to try magic to combat a society rooted so much in untenable premises about race. My hope is that even in an age in which we are all acknowledged misreaders and all careful to abide by Jean-François Lyotard's strictures against totalizing discourse, some of our student readers, whatever their culture, can become more aware of that culture's inscribed assumptions, of how axioms become internalized, and of how axioms can be made available for analysis. This awareness can result in a keener appreciation of the texts, like *Native Son*, that we and our students produce and are produced by.

NOTE

I want to thank my own cultural and reader response critics for their many invaluable suggestions on how to improve this essay: Randall C. Davis, Cynthia Felgar, Ken Guthrie, Jeri Holcomb, Lisa M. Williams, as well as the participants in my 1989 and 1991 Summer Seminars for School Teachers, which are funded by grants from the National Endowment for the Humanities.

On Women, Teaching, and *Native Son*

Farah Jasmine Griffin

No matter how I try to teach *Native Son*, my students inevitably return to Wright's treatment of women. My initial reluctance to focus on Wright's women emerged from several sources, the most important of which is my own ambivalence about the text in this regard. For years, when I was a student, my discomfort over Wright's portrayal of women, particularly black women, struggled with my conviction that the novel was significant as a literary and cultural text. Once I started teaching the novel, it was apparent that I had not yet settled this internal dispute. I would spend class time either focusing only on the issue of Wright's sexism or trying to divert my students' attention to other aspects of the text. The former approach always left me feeling that I had cheated the novel; the latter, that I had cheated the students.

Subsequently, I have sought to strike a balance—to find a way to acknowledge my anger and discomfort, and in so doing to validate theirs, without dismissing the text as unreadable because of its unsettling sexism.

I have taught *Native Son* in two types of courses: an introductory survey of African American literature and a more specialized, upper-level course titled African American Literature and the City. I have taught *Native Son* in three colleges—all of them small eastern liberal arts institutions. The student bodies are predominantly white, upper-middle and middle class. Few of the students are from large cities. My classes, however, are usually evenly divided between black and white students—a composition rare in these schools, where black students are easily outnumbered in most courses. Because two of the schools were all female, women outnumbered the men; in those classes, male students who attended an area college cross-registered for the course. At the coed college, the class was almost evenly divided between men and women. Most of my students were completely ignorant about the kind of environment from which Bigger emerges.

Initially, I had anticipated problems in presenting the text to white students. I expected them to cast Bigger as a sort of black Everyman, the essence of black maleness. Surprisingly, that has not proved to be the case. My white students almost too readily accept the notion that Bigger Thomas is a creation of his environment. They are all too willing to read him as a victim of a racist society. In fact, most of my white students see him as another kind of stereotype—a person completely devoid of agency. They dislike him, are afraid of him, yet somehow claim to have deep sympathy for him. They do indeed, except in one respect: his violence toward the women in the text—Vera Thomas, his sister; the white Mary Dalton; and the black Bessie Mears. This issue, usually first raised by a woman student, evolves into an unrelenting critique of Wright. Black women become very engaged in it, tearing into his descriptions of the black women in the text and his account of the rape and murder of Bessie.

At first, this direction, though anticipated and understood, veered me off the course of my reasons for having selected Wright's text as required reading. No other novel so effectively renders the black male migrant experience. Wright's work represents a turning point in the portrayal of African American life, and he establishes many of the tropes that others who follow him must accept or reject. Initially, I would present the work in this way, only to find my students giving me the "creature of his environment" line, which was followed by a critique of Wright's sexism. It was the pain and anger of my black women students especially that made me first confront my own pain and anger at reading any novel or story by Wright. These young women forced me to cease repressing those emotions. I had to share with my students the process of confronting anger while I explored ways in which the text itself provided a critique of Wright's sexism. This process is still incomplete, but I think it has made my teaching of the novel more effective. It has also given my students an understanding of the narrative that is more complex than surface readings allow.

We start with the notion of the social construction of Bigger. What are the elements that shape and influence this urban subject? On what levels does his construction occur? How does Bigger try to resist its negative effects? At what point in the narrative does Wright cease to objectively document this construction of Bigger and seem to fall victim to it himself?

To answer these questions, I turn the students' attention to three scenes in the text: the movie theater scene, the murder of Mary Dalton, and the murder of Bessie Mears. Together these passages illustrate how the dominant society constructs Bigger's desire and, by denying him access to fulfilling that desire, helps set the stage for his misguided attempts at creating an alternative fulfillment—the murders of the two women. The different language of each murder scene demonstrates the different responses that a black man, constructed as Bigger has been, has toward white and black women. Although in both instances it is a fatal response, in the first it reeks with desire and fear and in the second with anger and disdain. Wright eloquently portrays the manipulation of Bigger's desire, and he is critical of the violent turn of Bigger's frustrations, but he does not question Bigger's perception of women: white women as the embodiment of wealth, desirability, femininity, and power; black women as provincial, ignorant, and stifling. While Wright is aware of the mechanisms of urban power and their effect on Bigger, his critical consciousness has not allowed him to escape entirely the effects of these mechanisms on himself.

Movies and advertisements, bombarding Bigger with images of white power, white wealth, and white women, help create his desire for those things. Movies also provide images of black savagery and primitivism:

> Two features were advertised: one, *The Gay Woman*, was pictured on the posters in images of white men and white women lolling on beaches, swimming, and dancing in night clubs; the other, *Trader Horn*, was

shown on the posters in terms of black men and black women dancing against a wild background of barbaric jungle.   ([1966] 32)

Bigger and his friend Jack choose *The Gay Woman*. Initially they desire the white movie star sexually, but it soon becomes evident that the desire to possess her is linked with a desire to possess all that she represents for them. "I'd like to be invited to a place like that just to find out what it feels like," Bigger says. Jack responds: "Man, if them folks saw you they'd run. . . . They'd think a gorilla broke loose from the zoo and put on a tuxedo" ([1966] 33). Here the two images displayed on the movie posters have helped Bigger and Jack construct an image of themselves in relation to the dominant white society. The cinematic representation is one that Bigger desires; as a spectator he attempts to place himself in the picture on the screen. This fantasy moment is ruptured by his own understanding, reinforced by Jack, that there is no place for him in that world, that he, like the characters of *Trader Horn*, is no more than a savage beast. Like the gorilla in the tuxedo, Bigger does not fit, is awkward and out of place in the world portrayed by *The Gay Woman*.

Later, while viewing *Trader Horn*, Bigger saw

> pictures of naked black men and women whirling in wild dances and heard drums beating and then gradually the African scene changed and was replaced by images in his own mind of white men and women dressed in black and white clothes, laughing, talking, drinking and dancing. Those were smart people; they knew how to get hold of money, millions of it. . . . He remembered hearing somebody tell a story of a Negro chauffeur who had married a rich white girl and the girl's family had shipped the couple out of the country and had supplied them with money.   (36–37)

This paragraph is an excellent place for a close reading exercise. It demonstrates how Bigger's desire is created and shaped by the figures on the screen, how he attempts to reject the world of the jungle created for him by refiguring it as the white world and then creating a space for himself in the context of the white narrative. Whiteness is beauty, intelligence, and wealth. In Bigger's mind, possession of the white woman by the black chauffeur leads to possession of white wealth and therefore of a degree of white power. I have found the works of feminist film theorists Kaja Silverman and Mary Ann Doane especially useful in constructing a framework for reading this scene in *Native Son*. James A. Miller's essay "Bigger Thomas's Quest for Voice and Audience in Richard Wright's *Native Son*" is also useful for understanding the myriad ways Bigger tries to construct an alternative narrative. (I do not have my students read these theorists, I simply share the framework with them through my questions or lecture.)

I then point out the context of this narrative moment, which is book 1 ("Fear"). The class begins to explore the sources and nature of Bigger's fear.

One source is powerlessness. The fear leads to frustration, anger, confusion, and violence. The fear is also the fear of the migrant on the urban landscape. In "How Bigger Was Born," Wright tells us:

> The urban environment of Chicago, affording a more stimulating life, made the Negro Bigger Thomases react more violently than even in the South. . . . It was not that Chicago segregated Negroes more than the South, but that Chicago had more to offer, that Chicago's physical aspect— noisy, crowded, filled with the sense of power and fulfillment—did so much more to dazzle the mind with a taunting sense of possible achieve- ment that the segregation it did impose brought forth from Bigger a reac- tion more obstreperous than in the South.   (515–16)

The city sends the male migrant mixed messages. It provides him the space to fantasize about and helps him construct his desire for a world to which it de- nies him access. White women, representative of this world, are the vehicle through which it is accessed. Bigger the migrant brings with him from the South the taboo of interracial sex and the fear of acting on his desire, yet the city teases him by allowing a modicum of psychic space for his fantasies.

It is the fantasy and the fear that Bigger takes with him into the Dalton's home. Fear and desire fill the novel's first murder. He puts the drunken Mary to bed: "[H]e leaned over her, excited, looking at her face in the dim light, not wanting to take his hands from her breasts. She tossed and mumbled sleepily. He tightened his fingers on her breasts, kissing her again, feeling her move to- ward him" (96–97). Bigger has the courage to act on his sexual desire for Mary because she is only slightly conscious. It is a secret moment for him, one that many of my students call a rape because he touches her without her consent. Wright does not write the scene as a rape; in fact, he implies Mary's consent. In these days of heightened awareness about date rape, I find that more and more of my students see this touching as the rape of Mary Dalton. In class dis- cussion students may not only express anger at Bigger but also challenge Wright on the validity of a drunken woman's consent. This scene might be one of the first moments of the book where Wright is implicated in sexism. Of course, there will be students who agree that Mary desires Bigger as well. But Bigger has a position of relative power and authority at this point: Mary's safety is in his hands.

His momentary possession of power and desire is immediately disrupted and replaced with fear when Mrs. Dalton enters the room. Fear and desire culmi- nate in the enactment of a murder that is described in sexual terms:

> Frenzy dominated him. . . . Frantically, he caught a corner of the pillow and brought it to her lips. . . . Mary's fingernails tore at his hands and he caught the pillow and covered her entire face with it, firmly. Mary's body surged upward and he pushed downward upon the pillow with all of his

weight. . . . Mary's body heaved. . . . He clenched his teeth and held his breath. . . . His muscles flexed taut as steel and he pressed the pillow, feeling the bed give slowly, evenly, but silently. . . . He relaxed and sank to the floor, his breath going in a long gasp. He was weak and wet with sweat. . . . Gradually, the intensity of his sensations subsided. . . .
(97–99)

Unable to act on his sexual desire through intercourse, Bigger does so through violence—violence precipitated by the fear of being caught with a white woman. Mary is desirable to him because she provides access to the rights and privileges of a fantasy world constructed by the cinema. Unable to possess her, he kills her.

This murder is in stark contrast to the murder of Bigger's black girlfriend, Bessie Mears. When Bigger acts on his sexual desire for Bessie, it is a blatant rape. There is no consent; Bessie struggles and repeatedly says no. Yet he takes her violently, because her body is the only space where he can enact unbridled agency and authority. Shortly after her rape, he decides he must kill her, because only she can identify him as the murderer of Mary Dalton.

Bigger murders Bessie not in response to desire but in order to be rid of her. Bessie threatens to thwart his potential. She knows of his crime and, like all black women in Wright's texts, binds him to an inhibiting racial past. Bigger murders her not out of fear but out of the wish to be free.

Then he took a deep breath and his hand gripped the brick and shot upward and paused a second and then plunged downward through the darkness to the accompaniment of a deep short grunt from his chest and landed with a thud. *Yes!* There was a dull gasp of surprise, then a moan. No, that must not be! He lifted the brick again and again, until in falling it struck a sodden mass that gave softly but stoutly to each landing blow. Soon he seemed to be striking a wet wad of cotton, of some damp substance whose only life was the jarring of the brick's impact. He stopped, hearing his own breath heaving in and out of his chest. He was wet all over, and cold. How many times he had lifted the brick and brought it down he did not know. All he knew was that the room was quiet and cold and that the job was done.
(274)

It is significant that this murder takes place in the book titled "Flight." Bessie's death is a prerequisite to Bigger's freedom. The language describing her murder is not the language of desire and lovemaking; it is the violent sexual language of a rape. The rape precedes the murder, and the murder itself is an act of rape, a violation and destruction of a black woman. Bigger is not acting out of fear here; he kills Bessie out of hate—hate for what she as a black woman represents to him. Unlike Mary, she is not the future to which he aspires but the past from which he flees.

Though Wright is critical of Bigger's murdering Bessie, he seems to share Bigger's view of the black woman as a fetter, as a chain to the provincial past. There is no evidence that Wright is aware of the mechanisms that shape this perspective. While he details the elements of the dominant society that construct Bigger's desire for Mary, he does not detail those elements that construct Bigger's disdain for Bessie. Nor does Wright give the reasons why Bessie or Mrs. Thomas lives in a state of resignation. (Ann Petry, Wright's contemporary, gives reasons for resignation in her novel *The Street*. I usually assign it immediately following *Native Son*.) Although Wright is adept at revealing the social sources of Bigger's sexual attitudes, he has not escaped this socialization in his own life.

Just as Bigger sacrifices the lives of Mary and Bessie for his fear and freedom, so does Wright. Neither woman is given the complexity or depth of Bigger; they exist only to demonstrate Bigger's aspirations and inhibitions. Their murders and the following attempts to flee the police are the only instances where Bigger is allowed any agency. It is through these murders that he gains a heightened critical consciousness.

My students have taught me that there is no escaping Wright's blatant sexism and that in fact it constructs the novel almost as much as do Wright's political sensibilities. However, I am convinced that the text continues to be one of the most significant novels of the twentieth century. If there is no escaping his sexism, there is also no escaping the value Wright has rendered in the creation of Bigger and Bigger's fictional landscape. Instead of avoiding the woman question, I have found it useful to put that question on the table at the very beginning. And I have kept that question continually engaged in the matrix of power, desire, fear, and agency that maps Bigger's world.

When the murders of Mary and Bessie are presented to students in the context of power, desire, fear, and agency, the students' critiques of Wright's sexism become more complex. They can express their anger and pain without denying the complexity of the text or the astuteness of Wright's ability to portray so effectively the fears and frustrations of his urban black male protagonist.

Teaching Interculturalism: Symbiosis, Interpretation, and *Native Son*

James C. Hall

He did not think enough of them to feel that he had to; he did not
consider himself as being responsible to them for what he did. . . .
He felt that same way toward everyone. As long as he could remember, he had never been responsible to anyone. The moment a
situation became so that it excited something of him, he rebelled.
That was the way he lived; he passed his days trying to defeat or
gratify powerful impulses in a world he feared.

"This is a beautiful world, Bigger. . . ."
—Richard Wright, *Native Son*

Native Son often makes its way onto reading lists out of the progressive instinct
of teachers to diversify classroom discourse and to recognize and promote multiple world perspectives. It can be a great frustration, then, for teachers to encounter a quiet, even subdued, response to their efforts to generate meaningful
discussion. The great pedagogical problem that *Native Son* presents is the belief
of students (and many teachers) that this is someone else's text, someone else's
story. Threatened by Wright's cosmology, students claim aesthetic, political, and
cultural distance. My purpose here is not to deconstruct or psychoanalyze this
desire but to suggest some strategies for thwarting it. In particular, I want to
offer interculturalism as an aesthetic and an ethic, a hermeneutic that demands
of students recognition of the ways in which Wright's text implicates all readers.
While interculturalism makes great use of the biological concept of symbiosis,
the interdependence of life systems, it does not level cultural difference. In fact,
interculturalism signals the end of universalism and seeks to head off readings
that interpret *Native Son* in terms of general—and ultimately banal—concepts
like freedom and struggle. Wright's text requires that readers carefully work out,
through close reading and dialogue, patterns of responsibility. Interculturalism
seeks to demystify difference, so that extended and complex discussions of
African American aesthetic accomplishment can take place and so that conditions of social change can be grounded in the literature classroom.

Interculturalism, Cultural Criticism, and African American Literature

My use of interculturalism is based on a reading of the theoretical writings
of the Japanese architect Kisho Kurokawa, who has been at the forefront of a
movement to constructively mix elements of traditional Japanese culture with

elements of Western modernism. A both-and as opposed to an either-or ethic and aesthetic, interculturalism is related to postmodernism in its appreciation of collage and pastiche. But Kurokawa sees interculturalism as much more critical of the status quo than postmodernism. Cultural mixing is the inevitable product of postmodernity, but interculturalism highlights the transgressive nature of such boundary crossings. The selection of elements in the making of a text will inevitably lead to a multivocal and polyvalent construction, but this process is not value-neutral. Interculturalism emphasizes interpretation and perspective. As Kurokawa states:

> We are living at the start of an age of symbiosis in which we will recognize each other's differing personalities and cultures while competing; in which we will cooperate while we oppose and criticize each other. . . .
>
> (9)

The paradigm of interculturalism is ideal for negotiating the demands of the classroom. It accepts cultural and political difference as an inevitable part of history and of the process of reading, and it reconfigures interpretation as pleasurable, challenging, and productive.

For scholars of black cultural traditions interculturalism locates in African American literature a significant reservoir of both cultural criticism and aesthetic accomplishment. By highlighting the text's conjunction of disparate elements, it locates in African American expressive culture refinement and aesthetic excellence and preserves the agency of individual artists. By highlighting the ways in which reading is dependent on perspective, it is an effective tool for illustrating and challenging differential relations of power. This double duty suggests a way around the historical roadblock of oppositions between art as art and art as protest; it ignores neither the unique social conditions of African American experience nor the attainment of beauty in African American expressive culture. Interculturalism turns the teaching of African American literature into an exercise in cultural criticism and redefines this "minor literature" as central to the practice of English. (See Deleuze and Guattari on the characteristics of a minor literature.)

Native Son *and the Classroom*

My working assumption is that all classrooms are diverse and subject to the psychosocial phenomenon of "othering." While the pedagogical problem I have mentioned with regard to *Native Son* may be heightened when the classroom is mostly white and the tendency exists to rely on a few black students to provide both exegesis and testimony, interculturalism demands that we assume multiplicity. As Albert Murray suggests, American culture is a profoundly mulatto creation. In class discussion of *Native Son*, intracultural or intraracial disputes inevitably emerge, and they are often the more challenging because unexpected

—especially when some students see Bigger Thomas as an inappropriate representation of black racial identity or of African American masculinity. *Native Son* works on the reader as a narration of racial difference but also of class, gender, education, and ideology. The black text is, after all, polyvocal and subject to interpretation. Like the institutional, political, and cultural construction of a classroom, the meaning of *Native Son* is not transparent. This is not to enter the worn debate about protest literature; this is, instead, to take the figurative seriously.

I have found that one of the best ways to handle this multiplicity within a multiplicity is to highlight textual situations that seem to have a close relation to our classroom crisis of knowledge and desire. An extended discussion of problem areas can create a sufficient climate of trust and understanding to make possible more particular discussions of ideology, style, biography, history, or meaning. Such a preliminary discussion foregrounds interculturalism by showing students how they are bound by a text and how they can transcend its historical limits through understanding. If the ground is not properly prepared, teachers will struggle with a set of assumptions about the text and the institutional site of the classroom that students carry with them. Students may insist that *Native Son* is only about racism, is only about a past time, is only about the black ghetto, is only protest writing. Similarly, they may insist that in the classroom this text can be explained best or only by African Americans or by impoverished, uneducated, African American males (etc.) and that therefore it is best—safer—for them not to speak.

Henry Giroux argues that it is the responsibility of teachers to practice a critical pedagogy that directs student attention not only to the text but also to the process of the production of cultural meaning and to the politics of the educational institution (86–107). A critical pedagogy helps students recognize the ways in which the politics of a text may bear a close relation to the politics of a classroom. Drawing on the work of Paulo Freire, Giroux insists that in studying texts students are subjects and not objects; he points to "the need to interrogate how human experiences are produced, contested, and legitimated within the dynamics of everyday classroom life" (87). The contested site of the black text is crucial in this critical pedagogy:

> The knowledge of the "other" is engaged not simply to celebrate its presence, but also because it must be interrogated critically with respect to the ideologies it contains, the means of representation it utilizes, and the underlying social practices it confirms. At stake here is the need to develop a link between knowledge and power, one that suggests realizable possibilities for students. That is, knowledge and power intersect in a pedagogy of cultural politics to give students the opportunity not only to understand more critically who they are as part of a wider social formation, but also to help them critically appropriate those forms of knowledge that traditionally have been denied to them. (106)

Crossing Borders: Exploration and Transgression

A central and crucial element of plot in *Native Son* is the effort of the young whites Jan and Mary to investigate African American culture. Alternately good-willed and painfully naive, they express and act out the desire to know the culturally other. Students recognize that this desire is dangerous. If the novel suggests that such exploration may or must lead to violent confrontation, how can a classroom teacher expect an open exploration of the black text? Bigger Thomas's murder of Mary Dalton occurs as a result of both desire and a knowledgeable reading of the cultural implications of his being found in her room. If Bigger's exploration of the white female body, like Jan and Mary's desire to know African American culture, is a priori a violation, how can we expect any significant feeling of community to emerge? How can we expect students to speak when the text seems to advise doing otherwise? It is important for teachers to understand that students' confrontation with the world that Wright has created (or revealed) is, like Bigger's, fraught with fear.

Whatever the pedagogical agenda—an introduction to Wright, African American literature, or African American naturalism; a skills or process orientation to composition; or a more general encounter with interpretation and reading literature—a close reading of the two central border crossings in the text is a necessary first step to meeting other needs. This reading should create the conditions that make possible a constructive interpretive community to emerge. Of course, such a reading can be difficult to achieve. A mix of techniques is needed to account for multiple needs. Student writing—whether in response to the novel, to promptings from the teacher, or to other students—may be needed to set up an extended discussion of the text and its social transgressions. As we have come to understand that writing is best thought of as process, so we must think of reading or interpretation in a sophisticated way. But, again, although an investigation of border crossings in *Native Son* should lead to an effective and just classroom discussion of difference, it is still necessary for teachers to work to provide a safe atmosphere. Beverly Daniel Tate has excellent suggestions toward this end (3–4).

It would be imprudent for me to offer a model discussion or list likely responses. What I can suggest is a number of points of contention that might help teachers order their pedagogy. With regard to Mary and Jan's relationship with Bigger, a close reading organized around the following points may prove successful:

Cultural geography   Part of the drama of the encounter of Bigger, Mary, and Jan is the easy crossing of urban borders that designate space as black or white. Consider the cultural geography of Chicago—or of any major American city. Bigger experiences fear and trepidation as he prepares himself to go "among white people" (47). Wright's text identifies neighborhoods as white or black. How are we educated about the geography of urban neighborhoods? What is the source of the authority of this territoriality? Is it appropriate for

Mary and Jan to insist that Bigger take them to an authentic black restaurant? Why do they desire a "*real* place" (78)? Is Bigger comfortable with this crossing? What is the source of Jan and Mary's confidence in making this crossing? Where is their fear?

The discussion of physical borders should appear analogous to what is said and unsaid about classroom cultural territoriality. The discussion places on the table the issue of what belongs to whom and on what authority such possession relies. The issue, of course, is in no way settled. *Native Son* does not make clear if the appropriate strategy is to challenge all cultural and social divisions or simply to make them more just. The polyvocal text says only that such borders are acknowledged as having meaning. Students prove extraordinarily astute in assimilating this knowledge and using it to govern their own inquiries.

Social space   Jan and Mary insist that Bigger sit between them in the front seat of the car (77). What formal or informal rules are being broken? Is their sitting close together a substantive challenge to an unjust system of social mores, or is it merely a violation of etiquette? Is Bigger Thomas ready for such familiarity? How does this invasion of physical space compare with the interrogations of him by Mrs. Dalton (68–69) and by Mary and Jan (84–85)?

Highlighting the violation of social space is an effective way of stressing the need to distinguish between social knowledge and personal experience. That distinction can indicate to students the realm of the private. A discussion of *Native Son* is not necessarily an invitation for some people (students or teachers) to interrogate others about their identity or politics. Students, interested in this question, will often talk about how such information can and should be shared.

Social convention   What are we to make of Jan and Mary's open affection in front of Bigger (89)? (They may even be having sexual intercourse in his presence. That passage was cut from the 1940 edition.) Is this an honest effort to demonstrate or request familiarity? How does it compare with Jan's shaking of Bigger's hand (75)? Bigger responds to the handshake in this way: "He felt he had no physical existence at all right then; he was something he hated, the badge of shame which he knew was attached to a black skin. It was a shadowy region, a No Man's Land, the ground that separated the white world from the black that he stood upon" (76). How can a good-natured gesture result in this negativity?

The question here is the appropriateness of openness and its effect on others. How can certain actions often seen as expressing comfort or solidarity actually deny the individuality or even humanity of someone else? How do we know what actions are permissible in seeking to establish ties across cultural, racial, or ethnic borders? Issues of social space and convention provide an opportunity for students to discuss what can be assumed about a person's experience from a superficial reading of that person's appearance or from some single piece of knowledge, such as their religion or nationality.

The desire to know   What are we to make of Mary's statements expressing her desire to know more about African Americans and African American culture? She says (in the following passage, the first spaced periods show ellipsis, but the rest are original to the text):

> "You know, Bigger, I've long wanted to go into those houses . . . and just *see* how your people live. You know what I mean? I've been to England, France and Mexico, but I don't know how people live ten blocks from me. We know so *little* about each other. I just want to *see.* I want to *know* these people. Never in my life have I been inside of a Negro home. Yet they *must* live like we live. They're *human.* . . . There are twelve million of them. . . . They live in our country. . . . In the same city with us. . . ." her voice trailed off wistfully.
> (79)

Are her statements so painfully naive so as to become offensive? How else could they be put? And how could such questions be pursued?

The desire to know is of the utmost pedagogical (and social) value. The desire must be at the center of any discussion of the contemporary implications of Wright's novel for the diverse American classroom. I would argue even that the question is paradigmatic for an African American literary pedagogy. Should inquiry be directed, even propelled, by the individual desire or need for knowledge? What alternatives are there?

A close reading of Bigger's encounter with Jan and Mary leads to a more comprehensive intercultural pedagogy and a fuller discussion of *Native Son's* aesthetic accomplishment and cultural legacy by encouraging students to use the novel to interrogate their own reading practices. It also leads to discussion of the explosive question of the intersection of racial and sexual politics. If Jan's and Mary's inquiries and Bigger's response to them provide an opportunity to discuss cultural structure, another border crossing in the novel provides an opportunity to investigate the ideological and mythic suppositions of American cultural relations. For teachers organizing a reading of Bigger Thomas's sexual and violent encounter with Mary Dalton, the following questions are useful:

Trust and consent   Is Bigger's exploration of Mary's body to be understood as an accurate interpretation of Mary's wish for his friendship and for knowledge of the other? The text presents us with a troubling scene:

> He tried to stand her on her feet and found her weak as jelly. He held her in his arms again, listening in the darkness. His senses reeled from the scent of her hair and skin. . . . He stared at her dim face, the forehead capped with curly black hair. He eased his hand, the fingers spread wide, up the center of her back and her face came toward him and her lips touched his, like something he had imagined. He stood her on her feet and she swayed against him. . . . She tossed and mumbled sleepily. He

tightened his fingers on her breasts, kissing her again, feeling her move toward him. He was aware only of her body now. . . .   (96–97)

What is the relation between Bigger's previous experience with Jan and Mary and his use now of his advantage? Does Bigger's disadvantage as a member of an oppressed class make acceptable his transgression? Is that membership the source of his transgression?

This is volatile material. The current lack of consensus on American campuses about consent in matters of sexuality—to say nothing of the charged history and mythos of interracial sexuality—will be a great challenge to teachers. It is crucial, however, that students have some opportunity to explore difficult ways that race intersects with other discourses. How should ethical questions be pursued in the presence of such intersections? Can a single principle governing behavior be discerned?

The obvious and the unsaid   Why does Bigger respond as he does to Mrs. Dalton's sudden presence (97)? Why can't he simply explain the situation? What *is* the situation? What knowledge does he possess about black-white relations that makes him panic? Is his fear irrational? What are the implications for the classroom of Bigger's lack of faith in rational discussion?

These questions allow an airing of the historical and contemporary mythologies and taboos that often impede the formation of an interpretive community. Clearly the class must proceed not with the hope of banishing such cultural baggage but, instead, with the hope of acknowledging its tenuous relation to any kind of truth and its tendency to inhibit frank discussion.

While student responses to the above points will vary in political positioning, aesthetic concern, and especially interpretive self-confidence, a class can confront the danger and the limitations of the desire to know or express solidarity with the other. More important, discussion can suggest that violence is not the necessary result of intercultural exploration; violence is, rather, the result of unexamined relations of power and the failure to understand consent and trust, the difference between personal and the collective. The value of this process is that it both defines and limits community. It gives students some sense of the safety and danger of the particular institutional situation in which they find themselves; it gives them some idea of how to speak.

Other Intercultural Concerns: The Contested Grounds of the Text

Building on the groundwork laid in the discussion of border crossings, I move to a reading of the newspaper accounts of Bigger's crime (238–39, 256–57, 281–83, 296–97). These accounts provide an excellent opportunity for students to see the need for ethical reading (and writing). What is the relation between the newspaper words and the community's action? How is Bigger defined as beast, and how is such sensationalism an inhibitor of rational and knowledgeable interpretation? How is bad reading at work here? The interculturalist aesthetic-ethic also allows students to participate in the critical debate about the quality of *Native Son*'s third book ("Fate")—the novel's peroration—and especially about the book's univocality. How is Max's long presentation bad talk, in the light of previous class discussion? What is the significance of Bigger's silence? Why would Wright purposely allow perspective to be skewed over this long final section of the book?

By beginning to interrogate the character of borders in *Native Son*, the classroom community will encounter the ways that Wright has asserted the value of rational discourse, effective interpretation, and appropriate cross-cultural investigation. Responsibility (or the lack of it) plays an important role in Wright's America. The novel articulates a symbiotic approach to the understanding of social life, while simultaneously suggesting that such understanding is a possible method of transcending all determinism and all universalism.

Good intercultural pedagogy requires that the heteroglossic text and the plural classroom both be highlighted. Racial difference need not and must not be either submerged or mystified. Interculturalism takes as central Gerald Graff's dictum to "teach the conflicts." There is no better way to suggest to students that they should take interpretation and politics seriously than to make clear not only the social character of academic politics but also the politics of the classroom. Most important, interculturalism is an effort to present difference in a nontotalizing manner. Difference is not to be seen as end or restriction and especially not as definitive of selfhood. Interculturalism posits *Native Son* as a mirror in which a diverse student body sees diversity.

The Covert Psychoanalysis of *Native Son*

Leonard Cassuto

The most common—and probably the most effective—strategies for teaching *Native Son* harness two angers, Bigger Thomas's inarticulate rage and the tangled feelings of the reader of the novel, especially one who is meeting Bigger for the first time. Given his stated aim in writing *Native Son*, Richard Wright would surely not have been surprised if he could have seen how the book's anger can be used in the classroom. Paul Newlin observes that the "apolitical, good-kid, college student" population continues to be hit very hard by Bigger (140). Bigger, he says, stands as a blow to the youthful belief in a heritage shared by all of us, black and white (142). Anger at Bigger's deeds competes with anger at the system that made him. Debate over what to do about him leads to discussion of the social forces that made his behavior possible. Trying to understand Bigger in terms of the society that he inhabits is an approach that has been undeniably useful, tested over time in countless classrooms.

The rage in *Native Son* is like a tree trunk that can be followed out along numerous possible branches. But what happens when the anger is not there? I've found that Bigger doesn't always infuriate in the big-city classroom—he's too well known and too well recognized, and his audience has been at least partly desensitized to the shock he can bring. What if students have become so familiar with the Biggers of the world that they reflexively sympathize with the novel's Bigger despite his horrifying deeds? What happens when you face a class who wants to understand, feel for, and sometimes even root for Bigger through all his rage, hatred, and fear?

Faced with such groups in my Fordham University classes, I've found an answer by following the anger along one of its branches, the branch that leads to the study of Bigger's hatred and fear on the level of individual personality. Specifically, I try to spur my classes to find out who Bigger is as a person as opposed to a type. Seeing Bigger as a person with motives worth examining requires tools with which to examine them. For these tools I turn to psychoanalysis—only I don't tell my students I'm doing so until after they've done it with me.

The effort to know Bigger as an individual rather than an archetype can be problematic. It is certainly easier to experience *Native Son* on a social level, to confront the visceral response that springs virtually unaided from most people's reading of the book. Bigger's behavior demands that we ask what Bigger means to us in light of our membership in a social group that includes him. If his archetypal quality forces us to see him as a social phenomenon, then we need not acknowledge that he is an individual. To do so requires an extra interpretive step.

The archetypal qualities of Wright's characters have received a great deal of critical attention over the years, most of it negative. Of course Wright meant his creations to be viewed this way; Bigger Thomas's very name has a ring of the everyman to it, with its echoes of "Nigger" and "(Uncle) Tom" and all the historical resonance of that epithet. Even so, critics have complained about the flatness of characters envisioned as types; the strong implication is that they don't stand up to scrutiny. Harold Bloom, to pick a well-known example, complains that "Bigger Thomas can be said to have become a myth without first having been a convincing representation of human character and personality" (*Richard Wright* 2). Bloom suggests that Wright suspends Bigger between determinism—which would turn him into an ideogram—and choice, which would require him to be a fully realized human being. The flaw of *Native Son*, Bloom says, is that Bigger is neither (4).

My teaching experience leads me to disagree. We *can* view Bigger as a person, even as we take his everyman qualities into account. I think that this approach has been too hastily dismissed, for it certainly works in the classroom. My classroom experience further suggests that getting to know Bigger as an individual (a "possible person") complements what we learn about him in social context. An understanding of his conflicting drives makes him more credible when we look at him through the lens of society.

Paradoxically, it is the much attacked everyman aspect of character in *Native Son* that makes it a good psychoanalytic teach. The reason is simple: Freud was also writing about everymen and the desires that they (we) all have. His ideas thus yield surprisingly useful insights into a character who isn't supposed to have any depth. Wright describes Bigger's existence as a continuing effort "to defeat or gratify powerful impulses in a world he feared" (47). To Freud, this passage might describe us all. Bringing Freud's vision to bear on Wright's art informs the work of both—and is a useful interdisciplinary confluence for sophomores to take with them to future classes.

Psychoanalysis seeks to understand the mysteries and conflicts of desire. Bigger Thomas is pure desire, desire practically unmediated by reason. Wright describes how Bigger craves sensation and how his behavior is essentially a series of responses to that desire. Bigger fairly cries out for psychoanalysis. That he has received next to none is an interesting gap in the critical literature. More important, this elemental quality of Bigger's desires means that he can easily be psychoanalyzed by students relatively new to in-depth literary study.

My own desire is of course to hold class on *Native Son* and not on Freud. Even so, the risk of slipping into a lecture on psychoanalysis is ever present. I teach *Native Son* to sophomores of all majors in a required interdisciplinary, core-curriculum seminar that I focus on literary Darwinism. The course reveals and explores in literature the basic conflicts that Darwinism forced the intellectual world to reexamine (such as the opposition of both environment and heredity to personal will). *Native Son* is read near the end of the course, when I have begun to unify and sum up the semester's journey. It follows *McTeague, The Sea Wolf, L'Assommoir, Sister Carrie, The House of Mirth,* and other books. I generally spend a week on each novel. Over half my students are "nontraditional"—that is, adults returning to school. A few have been reading seriously for years and so can be quite sophisticated, but most are looking closely at evolution for the first time in any context. Almost none have read Freud.

The problem, then, is how to psychoanalyze Bigger without a lengthy disquisition on id, ego, and their associated discontents. Bringing psychoanalysis to bear on literature in a classroom of relatively inexperienced students can threaten the focus of discussion. It takes time to explain Freud's triadic metaphor, especially since students bring with them a lot of popular misconceptions about Freud. Disabusing them is certainly a worthy task, but a discussion of *Native Son* is not the place for it; the novel can easily be forgotten in the process. Moreover, jargon inhibits thought, especially when it is new in the mind and on the tongue. I budget only three hours for the text, so there is no time to explain the terminology of psychoanalysis. I therefore adopt a covert approach, a "cloak and blackboard" method in which I slip Freud into the discussion without mentioning him by name for a long time. This is nothing more than an applied introduction to psychoanalytic ways of thinking without the accompanying Freudian apparatus. I try to lead a discussion that results in students' considering division in the mind, conscious and otherwise. In other words, I offer the use of the theory without the label.

This tactic is possible because students already know a lot about Freud's ideas, often without knowing that they do. On his way to America for the first time in 1909 to deliver a series of lectures, Freud joked that he was bringing us "the plague." He was right, in a way: psychoanalytic thought has certainly proved contagious. Psychoanalysis has incorporated itself into our worldview to the point where it can be absorbed without being directly studied. When I read Freud for the first time as a beginning college student, I was not alone among my classmates in being struck by the familiarity of many of the ideas. Americans grow up accustomed to viewing certain desires as irrational, with roots that extend back to childhood. Everyone is aware of the Oedipus complex, even if many are skeptical of it.

A teacher can draw on what students understand of the psychoanalytic worldview from their participation in popular culture. Thanks to the psychopaths of the true-crime story and the TV cop show, the popularity of various therapy techniques, and myriad other allusions to and depictions of the divided mind, most people recognize the existence of the unconscious, even if they don't know what it's called.

I ask my students to analyze Bigger according to what they know about the unconscious. Wright puts Bigger's restless desire on display from the beginning of the novel. It comes out in Bigger's own words (" 'What you want to happen?' 'Anything,' Bigger said" [21]), in indirect discourse ("It was the old feeling . . . of wanting to grab something . . . and swing it into someone's face" [253]), and in simple description ("His entire body hungered for keen sensation, something exciting and violent" [39]). Students should see that Bigger has no understanding of his feelings: "What did he want? What did he love and what did he hate? He did not know" (277). They should also see that for him, desire is intimately connected to sex, violence, and white people. All three converge in his feelings about Mary Dalton, whom he desires and hates at the same time.

Students need little prompting to follow Bigger's conscious urges back to their unconscious roots. They understand that they need to examine his personal history, to look for clues to his present in his past. For this approach to work, students must consider Bigger Thomas not as a typical black man from the ghetto (though Wright clearly depicts him as one) but as a particular member of that group. It is important for the class to see Bigger as the child of his mother and—especially significant—of his dead father, and as brother to Vera and Buddy. In short, they should see Bigger as a specific person with a specific family and specific responses to a specific past.

This can yield surprising insights. The last time I taught *Native Son*, a student suggested that as a child Bigger might have been sexually abused by his father. That there is no direct proof of such abuse is irrelevant. What is noteworthy is that the suggestion represents an attempt to make sense of Bigger in light of his development. It is a new way of looking at him, and a new place to look. More common interpretive attempts center on what Freud calls displacement, where the desire for one thing takes the place of the desire for another. I have asked how Bigger comes to rely on violence for pleasure and have consequently presided over several lively discussions about what kind of childhood he might have had and how it might have helped shape his character and desires. Students understand that such interpretive strategies begin with a scrutiny of childhood experience, and they naturally gravitate in that direction. (This line of discussion incidentally offers me an opportunity to recommend *Black Boy* to them.)

Imagining Bigger's upbringing in an essentially fatherless household frequently brings the Oedipal conflict into the discussion. One of my college professors once said, "When you have children, you realize that Freud was right." Although many of my students have children, some of their younger classmates are not far removed from being children themselves. Bigger's exchanges with his mother become interesting raw material for debate over how his personality (including his sexuality) might have formed and evolved. When she says to Bigger, "We wouldn't have to live in this garbage dump if you had any manhood in you" (7), students have different opinions about how Bigger might feel. And Mrs. Thomas's exasperated "Bigger, sometimes I wonder why I birthed you" (6) rarely escapes group discovery and scrutiny.

Bigger's treatment at the hands of his mother leads students to understand how one might love, hate, and desire someone at the same time. One usually fruitful exercise is to have students compare Bigger's relationship to his mother—coupled with the absence of his father and his evidently unresolved feelings for him (85)—with his complicated attraction to and hatred for Mary Dalton. Use of the 1993 uncut edition of the novel, which makes Bigger's sexual attraction to Mary more explicit, benefits the exercise.

This unconventional psychoanalysis culminates twice, in a thematic closure of discussion of *Native Son* and in a drawing back of the veil to reveal the Freudian machinery that lies behind it. Because I don't know the answers to most of the questions I ask in class, the analysis of Bigger has taken different directions over the few years I have led it this way. My class last term concluded that Bigger's problem was his invisibility, a conclusion that many critics (including R. Lee; Gibson; and most recently Newlin) have independently arrived at by examining the book from a social perspective.

That individually based and socially based inquiries lead to similar conclusions is worth dwelling on. Because Bigger is both a type and a character, the social arguments about him can and should be linked to the interpretation of him as an individual. Speculation about how Bigger Thomas the individual was formed will never stray far from consideration of the social policy that is so important and undeniably Wright's focus. The homespun psychoanalytic method allows Wright's concerns to be viewed from a revealing new angle that enables students to examine the psychological reality of the social situation that creates the character.

At some point during the class session (usually near the end, but once at about the midpoint), I pull the veil away and show the class how I have been using psychoanalysis to shape the questions I asked them; I then give a short lecture supplying the psychoanalytic names for what we've been talking about. This second conclusion, since it follows exegesis that actually used these ideas, tends to be contextual rather than introductory. Students understand the names better because they've already been introduced to the ideas. (I learned the importance of that order the hard way. I once tried introducing the terms *inductive* and *deductive* to a composition class before we looked at examples instead of afterward. The results were disastrous; students were confused throughout. The same principle is at work here: It's easier to learn the name of something that you already understand and know how to use.) My brief presentation gives a broad overview of the psychoanalytic idea and fills in any significant thematic gaps that the discussion of *Native Son* failed to cover.

The class thus gains an appreciation of the psychoanalytic method that might otherwise have been obscured by technical terms, general intimidation, and often-seen disagreement based on unfounded popular assumptions. Students come to appreciate the connection that Freud frequently made between himself and Darwin, the historical background for which I supply late in the semester. The psychoanalytic explanation also legitimizes (in a way) the inquiry they've been engaging in. Most important, they gain a sense of concreteness, a feel for the tool that they just used and that they can use again, I hope, on their own.

My goal is to fuse a psychoanalytic reading with the trenchant social themes of *Native Son*. I want students to feel a sense of power over theory, a feeling that will permit them to see it not as an intellectual adornment or an intimidating monolith but as a tool. This approach to theory in the literature classroom is by no means limited to psychoanalysis. Though the aspiring humanities majors in my class will find this approach to theory useful later on, all students can benefit from the general lesson: that it is better to use technical knowledge than to be used by it.

Native Son as Depiction of a Carceral Society
Virginia Whatley Smith

Richard Wright and the French theorist Michel Foucault are linked by their preoccupation with the analysis of the repressive mechanisms of society. They look at similar phenomena: Wright in a creative, artistic way, Foucault in a philosophical and analytical way.

In *Discipline and Punish*, Michel Foucault argues that the punishment of social offenders changed by mid-eighteenth century from public trial and spectacle to the enclosed prison and then by the nineteenth century to the penitentiary system of "surveillance and observation" modeled on the penitentiary panopticon designed in 1843 by Jeremy Bentham. No longer was the prison a mere place of detention; along with the incorporation of scientific theories of criminal justice, it became the site "par excellence" for "disciplinary subjection" of criminals to codes of behavior modification designed to produce their moral reform (231–32). This penal surveillance system, also adapted in the United States, failed in its intent of moral transformation; the carceral system, states Foucault, instead produced from its environmental conditions the second self of the criminal, the "delinquent" or "recidivist" self (238, 265). Moreover, Foucault suggests, networks that engage in discipline, observation, and surveillance—hospitals, schools, reformatories, military systems, and factories—are modifications of the panopticon designed for the penitentiary. At its highest level of simulating the ever-present, gazing eye, the government, with its "silent, vigilant, mysterious," and even "unperceived vigilance" of its citizenry, has ultimately transformed the state into a "carceral society" (280). Foucault's analytic and explanatory framework provides a vocabulary that teachers can use to help their students understand the world Wright creates in *Native Son*. What Foucault describes as the penal mechanism in *Discipline and Punish* is similar to what Wright describes as a carceral society in *Native Son*. The Black Belt of Chicago is a figurative panopticon penitentiary: it produces the criminal-become-delinquent Bigger Thomas, whose acts of revolution and whose subsequent death place him in a complex and problematic relation to this world.

In his examination of the birth of the prison, Foucault analyzes the social treatment of offenders from the mid-eighteenth century to modern times. Although he focuses on the object—the body and its subjection to punitive measures—he infers a human subject, a social offender, to whom society has responded. Society's response has been to devise ways to deter criminality: from public torture, dismemberment, and execution to enclosed penal systems in the early nineteenth century (10). Both the external and internal punishments meted out to the body of the criminal were supposedly equal to the degree of the crime. But, with mid-eighteenth-century reforms and then nineteenth-century scientific studies, the "technology of the body" as focus of public spectacle yielded to the "technology of the soul" as treatment by scientists and educators (30). In both cases, society's efforts to discipline, punish, and reform malefactors led to their codification as criminals so that they could serve as moral deterrents to others. Still, one result of the "last words of the condemned man" confessionals has been the glorification of criminals as heroes or the denunciation of criminals as antiheroes in the literary forms of broadsheets, death songs, true stories, and detective stories that now compose "criminal literature" as a genre (66, 69).

My approach to teaching *Native Son* and Wright's other works of fiction is that they are about crime and criminality; thus I label them "criminal fictions." Michel Fabre indicates that after Wright completed *Native Son*, he became involved in working with juvenile delinquents while writing a novel on the subject of juvenile delinquency (*Unfinished Quest* 271). But Wright's interest in criminality preceded *Native Son*; it is manifest in his unpublished novel "Tarbaby's Dawn," shortened and reprinted as "Almos' a Man" (1940), and in his collection of short stories *Uncle Tom's Children* (1938). In each of these southern stories, the black hero or heroine commits a crime against white society, which responds in the modes of eighteenth-century reprisal and spectacle: public torture, dismemberment, or execution. There are beatings ("Fire and Cloud" [164]; "Bright and Morning Star" [195]); lynchings ("Big Boy Leaves Home" [48]; "Long Black Song" [127]); sentences resulting in flight ("Almos' a Man" [107]; "Big Boy Leaves Home" [53]); and executions by gunfire ("Down by the Riverside" [102]; "Bright and Morning Star" [215]).

Remarks made in class about criminality and punishment in Wright's short stories serve to introduce students to *Native Son* as depiction of a carceral society. In *Native Son*, Wright extends his argument to the North, where the plantation is transformed into an urban ghetto.

To involve students in the perspective of Bigger's Chicago ghetto as a figurative panopticon penitentiary, I start with the scene in book 1 after Bigger leaves his rat-infested apartment. He loiters on the street to watch workmen erecting a poster that bears the picture of State's Attorney David A. Buckley now running for reelection:

> He looked at the poster; the white face was fleshy but stern; one hand was uplifted and its index finger pointed straight out into the street at each passer-by. The poster showed one of those faces that looked straight at you when you looked at it and all the while you were walking and turning your head to look at it it kept looking unblinkingly back at you until you got so far from it you had to take your eyes away, and then it stopped, like a movie blackout. Above the top of the poster were tall red letters: YOU CAN'T WIN!   (12–13)

The poster of Buckley with its caption and his pointing finger is a "punitive sign" cited by Foucault and one that reflects the "rule of perfect certainty," which warns Bigger that an equal degree of punishment will be meted out to fit the crime should he break the law (Foucault 94–95). The incontrovertibility of the state government's threat is later confirmed after Bigger accidentally murders the white heiress Mary Dalton and is captured. Buckley informs him, "[Y]ou're *caught*," and, "We got the evidence" of her burned remains (338). The equivalence of Bigger's punishment to his crime is also revealed in Buckley's conversation with Boris Max, Bigger's lawyer, when Buckley states that the "grave wrong" done to the "poor old parents" of the murder victim will result in their wanting to "see that his boy *burns*!" (339, 338).

The poster of Buckley has a secondary meaning. His white face and unblinking gaze symbolizes the "faceless gaze" or omnipresent, transparent, vertical eye of surveillance in Bentham's panopticon penitentiary (Foucault 200). The square of Bigger's ghetto is an adaptation of the surveillance prison—Bigger says living there is "like living in jail" (20)—and a prison mechanism of power controlled by white policemen, government officials, and citizenry to "prohibit [Bigger's] entering certain areas" (Foucault 18). Walls or metaphors of walls to restrict Bigger's movements across race, class, or gender lines occur in the forms of a bedroom curtain, his apartment, Cottage Grove Avenue (which separates his black ghetto from the Hyde Park home of the rich Daltons), the Daltons' front gate, and Mary Dalton's bedroom.

Students quickly note forms of prison surveillance in *Native Son*: for example, policemen patrol Bigger's neighborhood to deter such criminal activities as Bigger's plan to rob Blum's delicatessen. Hierarchically, the towering eye of the prison state is signified by Buckley, both figuratively in the poster and literally, when, at the jail, a visiting Buckley towers over a seated Bigger. And Buckley's representation as the ever-present, vigilant, punitive eye of the government is summed up by Buckley himself when he tells Max, "My job is to enforce the laws of this state" (340).

That Bigger's world is a carceral society is seen by Bigger's move from figurative ghetto prison to literal jail. The various forms of seeing and unseeing in the novel—sightedness, blindness, the averted, silent, or direct gazes—all relate to the penal surveillance mechanism in Bigger's world. For example, Bigger's response to Buckley's poster, according to eighteenth-century strategy, should mark his behavior as either criminal or virtuous. His response of scorn to the threat of incarceration emerges from his prior experience of reform school and its networking. Bigger knows about the "police-prisoner-delinquent" ensemble described by Foucault, who states that the prison environment fosters corruption, fear, and disloyalty among prisoners and between prisoners and law officials.

At this point in my discussion I have my students examine Wright's naturalistic techniques for presenting the preexisting conditions of Bigger's industrialized world that have made Bigger's recidivism inevitable. One condition, paradoxically, is the advent of criminology as a science. Emergent in the nineteenth century, criminology brought together psychiatrists, psychologists, educators, and judges to understand criminals as well as the nature of their crimes.

Criminology represents the vertical and collective eye through which Bigger is seen by his society. But Wright privileges the inverted gaze, that is, from below to above, by giving the novel's limited perspective to Bigger, who views his world both through his inner eye, the mind's eye, and through his outer eye, the physical eye. This inner-outer eye dichotomy allows Bigger's dual perspectives to indict society and its scientific methods as failures. Bigger's welfare record, his cumulative criminal biography, is proof of this failure (53). Students can be directed to Mr. Dalton's interrogation of Bigger, which reveals that at fifteen Bigger had become a social offender and gone to reform school (54–55). Now at twenty, his carceral experience has neither "[neutralized] his state of mind" nor "[altered] his criminal tendencies" (Foucault 18).

Bigger's loitering on the street corners or at the pool parlor or his pillaging of the South Side with his gang is symptomatic of the illness of idleness that social scientists have identified as a factor that promotes crime. But employment and unemployment, according to Wright, have to do with color, class, and definitions. Foucault says that forced labor as punishment and as curative—and as a means to enlist slaves—diminishes in an industrial society and is replaced by mechanisms of "'corrective' detention" (25). Bigger feels that he was penalized to live in a ghetto because of his color (black) and class (poor) long before he began to commit illicit acts against blacks or whites (Wright, *Native Son* 342). These racist-classist penalties are evident when Bigger insists to Mr. Dalton that he was wrongfully detained for stealing tires and sent to reform school (56). Detainment is repeated when Bigger's gang members are picked up as suspects in Mary's murder because of their color, class, and association with Bigger (344). Bigger's environment continues to be one unchanging repetition. His detention in reform school and release from it back to the same depressed conditions have not corrected or modified his behavior. Reform school has only exacerbated his rage, frustration, and criminal tendencies, which are reflected by his actions and expressed through his stream of consciousness.

Bigger is "forced" into labor by the welfare office (through his mother) and then by Mr. Dalton, who induces Bigger with money, the idea being that work as a chauffeur, a job lower than an airplane pilot to Bigger, will transform his soul and lead him to moral reform.

The case file from the welfare office is the link between the revolving door of the juvenile court and the final destination of the Cook County Jail. That Bigger comes from a violent environment, that his father was "killed in a riot" in the South (85; the killing is more explicitly expressed as a lynching in the film *Native Son* starring Richard Wright), that Bigger lives in a dysfunctional and impoverished family, and that he has been forced too early to become the male head of the household are preexisting conditions; by the opening pages of the novel, they have made his state of mind dangerous. The reform-school experience, petty thefts, and assault on Gus are only a prelude to the capital crime awaiting Bigger's destiny. Bigger's plot to rob Blum's, though self-thwarted, is an interim step. The team of scientists, psychologists, educators, judges, and the juvenile courts, the welfare office, Mr. and Mrs. Dalton, Mary Dalton, and Jan Erlone—all act in concert as a carceral network to, in the words of Reverend Hammond, convert Bigger's "soul" to their two opposing ideologies of Christianity and Communism (326). Bigger's prior "activities and efforts or achievements" (if one uses Raymond Williams's definition of "work" in its basic sense [335–36]) do not come under the category of work as paid employment until Bigger accepts the job as Mr. Dalton's chauffeur. The street scene in book 1 unleashes a maelstrom of reasons why he resents the limiting aspects of his carceral world. His suppressed anger is symbolized by the burning in his stomach and by the raging furnace into which he stuffs Mary Dalton's body.

Students can grasp Bigger's transformation from petty thief to murderer by examining a recurring pattern of plot and incident in Wright's criminal fictions. Note the following seven stages:

1. The scene opens with the hero enclosed by a visible or invisible four-cornered barrier (baseball diamond, field, house, region) and facing a strange adversary, strange ally, or familiar opponent. *Native Son* opens with Bigger and his family imprisoned in their ghetto apartment and facing a familiar opponent, a rat.

2. The hero has a psychological or physical battle with the adversary or ally. Bigger is attacked by the rat, but he kills it.

3. The hero interacts with his black or white community. Bigger argues with his family about money and the chauffeur's job, fights with Gus, meets the Daltons and later Jan Erlone.

4. The hero has an accident or makes an error in judgment that alters the course of his life. Bigger carries the drunken Mary Dalton to her room only to find that his chivalrous act has positioned him for discovery and charges of rape by Mrs. Dalton. He accidentally smothers Mary to death with a pillow, trying to keep her from revealing his presence.

5. The hero feels fear because of his error. Bigger fears, knowing that he is a dead man if caught. He sets a plan in motion to frame Jan Erlone.

6. The hero takes flight to outwit his opponents (physical and psychological). Bigger first takes psychological flight. He wants to experience to the fullest his newly attained self-empowerment and to control his destiny even though he knows it will be short-lived. When the police discover Mary's bones in the furnace, Bigger takes physical flight through the ghetto.

7. The hero confronts his fate—usually death and often by gunfire. Bigger is condemned to the electric chair for a rape he did not commit and a death that was an accident. He is never tried for raping and murdering his black girlfriend, Bessie Mears, whose body is used as circumstantial evidence to corroborate his criminality and indict him for Mary Dalton's murder.

Native Son opens with Bigger imprisoned in a square, his apartment, and concludes with Bigger in another square, his jail cell. The repetition of Bigger's prison environment is "regressive," as defined by James Snead, since the ending of the novel cuts back to Bigger's beginning status of enforced confinement. Nonetheless, the linearity of the novel's three-part structure shows that Bigger's psychological growth is "progressive" (Snead 59, 67). Bigger moves from dreaming to waking and from a nonbeing to an existential hero empowered by his own self-creation (Fabre, *Quest* 171). Close attention to these stages of plot development enables students to understand the contradictions arising from Wright's paired oppositions by race, class, gender, and so on: two races; two families; two spatial areas; two economic levels; two female victims.

Bringing out these dualities leads to other social oppositions. Bigger's game of "playing white" with Gus (18) is paired opposite to Mary Dalton's "playing Negro" with Jan Erlone (which shows how whites, whether rich or Communists, misread the text of the Negro). As the exploited laborer responding to the capitalist yoke, Bigger enacts the Communist fantasies of Jan and Mary when, after killing Mary, he steals the money from her purse and then attempts to extort ransom for her in retaliation against her capitalist father, who had charged Bigger's family excessive rents for a slum dwelling.

Neither of the Daltons ever sees Bigger as a human being; for them he is but another object of their scientific experiments in Negro philanthropy. Had the Daltons not been class-bound and color-blind, they would have noticed that their prize experiment, the black ex-chauffeur Greene, had side-by-side pictures of famous black prizefighters and famous white, blond Hollywood actresses displayed in his room. The Daltons do not read correctly their experimental data, for Greene, more blatantly than Bigger, coveted the forbidden white doll-woman—in the way one of his idols, Jack Johnson, did.

If the Daltons misread Bigger's text, the law does too. Bigger uses his reading of *Real Detective Story Magazine* to outwit the investigators; he employs counterdetective strategies of playing the shuffling, minstrel figure to reinforce their assumptions that Negroes are illiterate and lazy as commonly stereotyped. But the police miss the giveaway Black English Vernacular of "the letter say" in Bigger's ransom note, which should have alerted them to the race of the note's author (203).

The element of public spectacle in the scenes of Bigger's capture and trial, contrasting with the criminal justice system's movement from outdoors to indoors, show how little social progress and social justice have occurred for blacks. The crowds of whites that prejudge Bigger as a rapist murderer, hurl racial epithets at him, and refer to him as a beast recall the brute level of eighteenth-century mobs that turned the punishment and execution of criminals into a sport. The theatricality in the three stages of indictment—inquest, trial, and sentencing—is Wright's method of emphasizing that society's denigration of Bigger has produced Bigger's second persona, the delinquent. The interrogations that begin with Bigger's encounter with the Daltons and conclude with Max's questioning of Bigger illustrate that society continues to avert its gaze even when it knows the truth of its guilt. Images of whiteness, from the characters to the cat to the snow, symbolize the forces that imprison Bigger and efface his blackness and thus his humanity. But in accidentally colliding with that white power, with those white laws and mechanized systems, Bigger finds at a basic level that his killing in the darkness of the night is his awakening into manhood and selfhood. He breaks out of prison mentally, making blackness empowering as he schemes to outwit his opponents. The irony is that Max, his Communist lawyer who has acted as his voice in a twenty-two-page propaganda speech at his trial, is too frightened to confront Bigger's humanity in the final scene of the novel—an extension of Bigger's "last confession." Bigger's assertion of his existential credo to Max, "But what I killed for, I *am*!" (501) is, as Foucault would say, "an outburst of protest in the name of human individuality" (289). And even if Max comprehends the Black English connotation of self-definition implicit in Bigger's unusual statement in Standard English, which is doubtful, he never conveys Bigger's confession to the courts or society, thereby suppressing it and thus ensuring that Bigger never rises as a human being or a social hero—as was the practice in the eighteenth century: to suppress the glorification of the criminal as hero.

In conclusion, Wright precedes Foucault, but Foucault expresses in *Discipline and Punish* what Wright elaborates in his criminal fictions, especially *Native Son*. Wright's depiction of a carceral society of surveillance, observation, and imprisonment in 1940 served as a warning that the penal system was producing recidivists like Bigger who would attempt to win their equal rights at any cost. Examining *Native Son* today, students are able to see that Wright's novel is prescient. Reading *Native Son* through the lens of Foucault's *Discipline and Punish* can deepen their understanding of Wright's critique of America.

Lessons in Truth: Teaching Ourselves and Our Students *Native Son*

SDiane A. Bogus

Given the multicultural, multiethnic face of today's American classroom, whether at the secondary, college, or graduate level, teachers of *Native Son* have found the novel not only a cultural anachronism to teach but also a monstrous classic: it poses problems for the presentation of the material as well as for the intrinsic message that any presentation of it—no matter what the critical approach—delivers. For more than fifty intellectually productive years, scholars and critics and, presumably, teachers of *Native Son* have been engaged in a dialogue that has included every imaginable critical approach. The most salient and self-perpetuating critical and popular discussions agree that in *Native Son* Wright captured for all time a hateful look at a racist and unjust society that can and does spawn unembraceable heroes like Bigger Thomas. Bigger's gruesome murders of two women and his bullying, disrespectful treatment of his family and friends, and of life itself, have intrigued the community of critical readers since Bigger first cursed aloud as he pounded the head of a rat in the opening scene of the novel.

Anger and bitterness are untoward emotions that poison the spirit and blind one to truth, and truth in *Native Son* is housed in a spiritually bereft black man who appears to be traditionally unredeemed by Christ yet who undergoes "conversion by murder" (Margolies, "Richard Wright"). Bigger's conversion needs a close reexamination, for in "creating" himself he has violated, with seeming impunity and without remorse, the sixth commandment and readers are asked to accept that violation in the name of fiction.

As a teacher and critic, I agree that the book is a most sobering reminder to American society—to white America especially—that as long as the struggle for justice and humanity continues, the plight of Bigger Thomas must be seen as representative of that struggle, no matter how many seasons of readers weave their thoughts into the fabric of the criticism of *Native Son*. Yes, Bigger Thomas is like us, if by "us" we mean American society at large. In the years since the novel's publication, the festering conditions that drove the symbolic Bigger to his crimes have not been ameliorated; instead, those years have seen the incidence of hate, prejudice, and discrimination grow.

This unhappy fact seems to validate what Wright saw in *Native Son* as a prophecy for the future of America. Given the ironic propinquity between the world of *Native Son* and contemporary America, one must realize that criticism has taken this novel seriously, has taken it as a "blueprint," to use Wright's word, for conditions real and dramatic, for circumstances significant and life-threatening. Agreed, *Native Son* is a prize, a monument to black artistry and perseverance, but as it once catered to, as Margolies has said, "the paranoid fantasies of racist extremists" ("Richard Wright"), it now reinforces the harsh and unbearable truths of modern American society and, indeed, of the oppression of people of color throughout the world. But criticism is one thing, teaching *Native Son* another.

What are we teaching or not teaching when we present *Native Son* to our students? Are we asking students to put the mirror of this novel to their faces and note the absence of a reflection? If so, why? And if not, why not? Are we asking students to negotiate our critical impasses or to posit theses for themselves about the meaning of the novel? Just how would they see Bigger if we didn't impose on them the intellectual and symbolic interpretations of years of reading? Are we insisting on their own discovery rather than on our studied and informed dialectic? If so, why? Or if not, why not? Finally, are we attempting to see a moral and spiritual imperative in *Native Son*?

These questions are only a beginning survey of the questions that haunt my teaching of *Native Son*. It is uncomfortable for me to stand authoritatively in front of a class of students and determine for them the rhetorical, symbolic, and considered dimensions of any novel. Such teaching has been a part of the way that I myself internalized the autocratic and systematic American-European literary point of view—and to some degree the implicit racism that favors white literary and cultural constructs while distorting, underrepresenting, ignoring, or undervaluing the constructs of my black world.

Native Son does little, if the traditional reading is employed, to counter the false or nonexistent images of black American life. It adds nothing estimable to contemporary letters and art except a once radical view of the merits of communism and a polemical rhetoric for social and economic justice. We've heard it all before, and communism is dying. I would not wish to pass on to my students subliminally some exalted analysis of the book (and of the character of Bigger) implying that his choices in life are in any way praiseworthy, nor would I want to confer the status of hero (even antihero) on him because he murders (*why* he murders is beside the point). I would tend to leave the analysis of the novel to class discussion, hoping that student views would approximate those of critics or, better, that the students would make discoveries heretofore unarticulated.

While I hesitate to direct student response to *Native Son*, I still need to collect, summarize, and then channel the divergent and unusual ideas that may emerge in a classroom. In the process of that channeling, no matter what my distance during a class discussion, students will not release me from the responsibility of stating an opinion. This causes me further difficulty. I feel I should not only share directly or indirectly an informed opinion of the novel but also question the validity of that opinion. Am I to offer a review of scholarship—positions taken by selected scholars—or my personal reading? Whatever I offer, I know that a word, a smile, a reference to a scene, a change of tone will be taken as a point of study; students will build their ideas and fashion their response to the novel around my stated or inadvertent assessments. Naturally, graduate students can more readily weigh opinions, dare to differ, or explore the germ of an idea further, but undergraduate students generally mark my opinion in a discussion, as if highlighting a major fact in a text. There-fore I control what can be genuinely taught, that is, transmitted: not ideas but lessons to live by. It is a great responsibility.

I perceive, too, that unless students (at any level) have had the good for-tune of previously reading this metaphorical epic—as Robert Bone has called it (*Negro Novel*)—their final assessment will be very close to those of their professor.

To secondary school and undergraduate students, *Native Son* speaks am-biguously about the importance of education and the responsibility of the teacher. Bigger enters the courtroom for his trial:

> He looked about. Yes; there were his mother and brother and sister; they were staring at him. There were many of his old school mates. There was his teacher, two of them.   (427)

Is Wright suggesting that these school kin, these classmates and teachers, were there for Bigger and he never knew? Or that, even though Bigger had only a grammar school education, school figured significantly in his life? With the sorely abbreviated glimpse Wright does give us of how Bigger grew up, it seems incredible to me that Bigger, who is said to "look like an intelligent boy" (351), who planned and executed countless petty crimes, who wrote the ransom note to the Daltons with enviable rhetorical proficiency, who read the newspaper ac-counts of his arrest and of his inquest and its decision, and who on the basis of only eight years of schooling had ambitions (and the mathematical aptitude?) to fly an airplane, could use his cognitive skills only for crime.

Bigger is not illiterate. He is not even functionally illiterate by today's stan-dards. But he tells Max, "I reckon I didn't want to do nothing" (409). In this light, he is a counterinstructive model to striving secondary school and undergraduate black students and to nonwhite ethnic students. His story is anti-intellectual to graduate students, and it misinforms all students about the historical times in which Bigger lives. It paints for students of color and white students an embar-rassing and fatalistic picture of failed black achievement. This negativism goes far beyond Wright's original discussion about his failure to paint "the best" of the black race (525). Students who are seeking education as a means of greater so-cial mobility and employment opportunities will know that Bigger did not even try to advance himself. This is one of the clearest points of the novel despite his (and Wright's) insistence that he has been denied opportunity:

> Why should I want to do anything? I ain't got a chance. I don't know nothing. I'm just black and they make the laws. . . . I wanted to be an avi-ator once. But they wouldn't let me go to the school where I was suppose' to learn it. They built a big school and then drew a line around it and said that nobody could go to it but those who lived within the line. That kept all the colored boys out. . . . I wanted to be in the army once. . . . Hell,

> it's a Jim Crow army. All they want a black man for is to dig ditches. And
> in the navy, all I can do is wash dishes and scrub floors. . . . I'd like to be
> in business. But what chance has a black guy got in business?   (409–10)

Bigger's blaming others, goofing off, stealing, being disrespectful to his
mother and family is excusable only if he does not see the error of his ways. But
it seems to me that Bigger does, and that he had the minimal educational tools
to begin to emancipate himself and did not, and therefore that he failed where
others succeeded and transcended. In the 1940s blacks were in fact being in-
tegrated into the national defense program (a march on Washington that would
have forced the issue was called off because whites complied with blacks' demands), and Benjamin Davis was appointed brigadier general. Meanwhile the
Supreme Court ruled favorably for black Americans in a railroad jim crow case,
showing that jim crow practices were under attack in this country. But most important, the first United States Army flying school for Negro cadets opened at
Tuskegee. *Native Son* should not be taught without these facts. The difficulty
for teachers, an ethical difficulty, is that these facts tend to undermine Wright's
controlling vision for the novel, the proposition that Bigger Thomas is the creation of wretched, insurmountable conditions.

Critics, citing what lessons are to be learned from *Native Son*, have often
said that it forces one to face "the truth about what man does to man" (Reilly,
Afterword 397). They say that it teaches, albeit badly, Marxist tenets. That it
provides a continuing opportunity to honor the African American writer who
was the first to probe the psychology of the disinherited generation of the
slums. What they don't say is that to teach *Native Son* one must also teach the
"speechless hate" that underscores every page. One must teach the utter despair and hopelessness of Bigger Thomas and the fatalism and economic de-
termination that congest, restrict, and control his life. Bigger cries out:

> I didn't want to kill! . . . But what I killed for, I *am*! It must've been pretty
> deep in me to make me kill! I must have felt it awful hard to murder. . . .
> What I killed for must've been good! . . . I didn't know I was really alive
> in this world until I felt things hard enough to kill for 'em. . . . It's the
> truth. . . . I can say it now. . . .
> (501; only the ellipsis after "kill for 'em" is original to the text)

Many critics see this speech as a major point of the novel. Am I to agree that
"Bigger's crimes can be seen as that which stands in the place of art. He has no
medium in which to work other than violence" (Johnson, "Re(a)d" 145)? Am I
to teach his crimes as his act of creating himself? Am I to teach that murder
can redeem, that the evils Bigger internalized from the evil white society were
such that he can stand redeemed of his act, redeemed within even if he must
die? I think not. I think the text embodies truths that can provide a more teach-
able reading.

The questions are endless, the possibilities inexhaustible for entry into the world of a novel like *Native Son*, but the primary question we scholars-teachers should ask is what we want our students to come away with from this adamant text. Teaching expectations, beyond a basic understanding of the central plot and its everlasting "prophecy of our future" (xx), depend on the ethnography of the class; on students' sense of a safe community of peers, which is necessary for their maximum participation in the dialogue; on the level of intellectual development; and on how well the text correlates to their lives and to their (potential) understanding and appreciation of American life and literature.

The problem with teaching *Native Son* is that one must bring from more than fifty years ago Wright's decidedly controlling point of view to the students. Many critics have said that the view of the unremitting third-person anonymous narrator who speaks for Bigger, no matter how qualified, updated, and redefined by critical analysis and pedagogical approach, will demand an introduction to the students. Teachers who take Wright to task for his incomplete portrayal of the black community as a whole or for his failure to give more than the most rudimentary sketches of his characters still are constrained to acknowledge the authorial intention in "How Bigger Was Born" and to accept, begrudgingly, the unimpeachable decision that Wright made to limit the novel to Bigger's thoughts and feelings for the sake of a heightened sense of realism.

Indeed, the realism is appalling when we think of the scenes when Bigger smothers Mary to death, when he chops off her head because she doesn't fit into the incinerator, and when he kills Bessie with sodden blows to the head after using her body sexually. These scenes disturb the gentle and gratify the perverse, much like the horror films that contemporary moviegoers avoid or attend. But because Bigger's crimes are murders, they are not acceptable to the law or to us as readers, even if seemingly justified by the text. I do not believe they are in truth justified or that they are the sine qua non for Bigger's conversion. They are only the catalyst for a redemption that is less obvious than most critics argue. The crimes lead Bigger to confront the ineffable idea of God and moral law, much as in the trial of Job, the faithful servant of God who was tried beyond endurance. Here the novel reverberates with a rarely discussed subtext: Bigger's conversion, which intimates a point of view in Wright more spiritual than religious (since Wright discards Christianity as a tool against oppression). This conversion creates and defines a less existential Bigger; it reveals a Bigger who has been goaded on by blind pride but redeemed by a fresh "[commitment] to faith" (321). It is from here and only from here that teaching *Native Son* is possible for me.

To read *Native Son* as I do, one must read, freely and with depth, the conversion scenes, that is, when Bigger is in his cell awaiting the inquest and trial. In these scenes his rejection of Christianity is not absolute; it does not entail a rejection of God or a search for faith—faith in himself if in nothing else.

Bigger's conversion does not depend on these considerations, although they cannot be excluded from his process of transformation. Bigger is a Job figure, a proud man who, having once placed his trust in God, must decide if that trust has been betrayed. Job and Bigger both complain of unwarranted trials of spirit and body, but unlike Job, who complains against God, Bigger complains against society. Unlike Job, Bigger is always afraid, whereas Job, a righteous man, knowing well the might and omnipotence of God, dares to question God's right to test him. Bigger never questions God, but he does begin to question himself. Ultimately, the similarity between Bigger and Job proceeds from their response to their trials: "Even today is my complaint rebellious / My stroke is heavier than my groaning" (Job 23.2). This quotation, which Wright used as the inscription for the book, suggests four views of Bigger's conversion. First, even after the unbearable trials that preceded his crimes and the literal trial for his life, Bigger is still suffering emotional pain, and he determines to fight against that pain because the trials were unjust. Second, Bigger has been broken by the stroke, or blows, to his spirit, for the blows have been and remain heavier than his groans of pain. In other words, he fights (rebels) only to stay alive. Third, Bigger's rebellion against his sufferings and trials will be (or has been) a thing of greater measure than the pain he endured, and his stroke of retaliation will be (or has been) heavier than any literal or figurative groan of pain he may have uttered. Finally, Bigger, like Job, has resisted and will always resist oppression from wherever it comes. Tests by pain and suffering will always leave people like them determined to fight back. Whichever view one takes, it is clear that Wright has chosen some scriptural or spiritual message as a guiding principle for the book. The inscription bears our scrutiny, and other scholars' scrutiny, because it speaks to the fight Bigger has with the idea of responsibility and to the justification for his fate.

Bigger's moral or spiritual conversion begins in his cell when the black minister prays for him. Bigger recalls his religious teaching. Although he tries not to listen to the minister, he feels a guilt "deeper than that which even his murder of Mary had made him feel." He realizes that his "first murder" occurred when "he had killed within himself the preacher's haunting picture of life" (328). In this moment a Bigger who has never been present in the novel is born. A cause without true explanation is suggested. The effect so clearly articulated by Wright is Bigger's uncontrollable sense of fear, hatred, and shame. But suddenly, and subtly, he is not the Bigger of endless projections of hatred and shame but one who beneath that familiar and hardened exterior can feel more enlightening emotions, even the great sadness of having killed himself. With that first murder went his potential and the possibility of living in reasonable peace with the world, a world in which he could see himself as human, as deserving a fair chance. Bigger's lack of faith, trust, and hope and his fear have kept him blind to the good that might have developed from growing opportunities in his life. He begins to see himself as he has been, not necessarily as the author wishes us to see him at the end—that is, as a victim of racism, deprivation, as a boy driven to murder by circumstances beyond his control. It appears that Bigger had the opportunity to free himself from the conditions that bound him, but fear, a fear that *he* generated against the world, locked him into a vicious circle of rebellion and rejection, resentment and mistrust. Now a murderer, and one without a clear understanding of his motivation, he finds it difficult to accept the specter of his failed responsibility to himself. In the scene with the minister, he attempts to harden his heart by telling himself that he did not fit into the preacher's story of Creation, that it excluded him, that he had tried to smother it when he killed Mary. He is afraid to allow himself to believe in this kind of redemption. He wants to be satisfied that his crime has "created a new world for himself," and he is resigned to die (264), yet the preacher's words penetrate and make him begin to feel.

After this spiritual or moral awakening, Bigger accepts silently the preacher's gift of a wooden cross around his neck. The cross, as a symbol of Christianity, might indicate that Bigger will be saved from hell if he repents his sins. But his silence is not repentance; it suggests a beginning acquiescence to feeling, to a deeper level of connection to himself and others. The cross represents the hereafter and possibly the unfailing love of God, but Bigger does not accept the cross for these reasons. He does not believe that praying to God ever got black people anything (412) or that church ever gave black people happiness.

Bigger's excuses for his lack of responsibility and faith in the world rest with his decision that he "never had a chance," but as he spends more time in his cell and as he must review his life, confronting each of several significant characters, from the preacher to his mother, from Jan to Mrs. Dalton, from the crazed inmate to Max, he becomes more and more aware that he has "gained a pinnacle of feeling upon which he [can] stand and see vague relations that he . . . never dreamed of" (418).

Bigger admittedly snatches the cross from his neck when he glimpses the burning cross of the KKK, declaring, "I can die without a cross. . . . I ain't got no soul!" (392), and rejecting the preacher's attempt to comfort him. For an overwrought moment Bigger believes that evil is more powerful than good because the cross of Christ, manipulated into evil uses, apparently can therefore mean anything or nothing at all. Having trusted the preacher, having allowed himself to begin to feel again, to think that the world might be different from what until now he had allowed himself to see, Bigger takes a step backward and resolves "never again to trust anybody or anything" (394).

But after his experience of this slight faith, or of simple trust, he cannot go back to what he was before. Each trial of Bigger's spirit readies him for the vision that will free him to believe, and to die. Although he professes no belief in God, he has grown in spirit, a growth that would not have been possible without these tests of his humanity. By the time Max comes to see him, he is "poised on the verge of action and commitment" (399), detached from his hate and fear.

Although most critics see Max as a political icon and as a white man who stands for Wright's refusal to completely condemn the white race, Max is a decent man, a Jew who knows the contours of racism and discrimination yet possesses a faith in humanity founded on a political ideology. He cannot sell Bigger that ideology, but inadvertently, in the first part of an extended metaphor about buildings and men's wishes to build and create (497–98) he does tell him something. After Max leaves, Bigger gains an awareness of his relationship to other human beings. His "will to believe" (422) becomes an essential motif for the teaching of this text. It suggests a moral or spiritual reading that can serve the moral and spiritual lives of students and teach them the importance of taking responsibility for themselves. It suggests, too, a path away from difference and alienation, a means to connect multicultural, multiethnic people in a classroom. Bigger's "new picture of the world" (422) is presented not without some ambiguity and hesitancy on Wright's part. Wright has Bigger vacillate: as Bigger rethinks his crimes, he tries to deny his fear of dying, to accept death stoically. What Bigger experiences is not a traditional religious conversion but an epiphany, a self-realization, an awakening. Interactions prompted by his mother's and Jan's need for consolation, the minister's prayer, Mrs. Dalton's forgiveness, the inquest, and Max's talk bring Bigger to a vision of himself as the equal of other men, to a vision of himself as a man. In sharp contrast to his previous shame, he gains a new sense of pride. This proud conversion to humanity is not without a "strong counter-emotion" to "leave this newly seen and newly felt thing alone" for fear it might take him back to "deeper hate and shame" (418), but Wright describes Bigger's arrival at a larger vision of himself in community with others (the ellipsis is original to the text):

> Another impulse rose in him, born of desperate need, and his mind clothed it in an image of a strong blinding sun sending hot rays down and he was standing in the midst of a vast crowd of men, white men and black men and all men, and the sun's rays melted away the many differences, the colors, the clothes, and drew what was common and good upward toward the sun. . . .   (420)

For the first time in his life Bigger comes to know the responsibility of living, but it is too late to undo what he has done. He cries, "I don't want to die" (421); knowing what he has failed to see, he must make peace with it in order to die. He wanted to "feel with as much keenness as possible what his living and dying meant. That was all the hope he had now" (489). When he sees Max again for the final time, he wants to share this process, to retrace his steps to self-realization and responsibility:

> Mr. Max, I sort of saw myself after that night. And I sort of saw other people, too. . . . Well, it's sort of funny, Mr. Max. I ain't trying to dodge what's coming to me. . . . I know I'm going to get it. I'm going to die. Well, that's all right now.   (496)

What Bigger means by "all right" is that he has killed in order to say "I am." He says, "[I]t must've been pretty deep in me to make me kill!" He felt that need "awful hard" and did not know he was "alive in this world until [he] felt things hard enough to kill for 'em" (501). This speech is not acceptable in the light of Bigger's conversion. His explication does not ring true, because he didn't really begin to feel until after he murdered. He didn't kill because he felt fear, shame, and anger or because of his need to be recognized as human; he killed when he was afraid. It is only after he kills that he becomes capable of more complex emotional responses to life; the simple animal-like instinctual responses of anger and fear are joined by a new pride, compassion, and moral soul-searching. Murder did not make him human. His acts of murder were inhuman, but they led him to a discovery of his humanity.

Bigger did not kill to find his humanity; he found the humanity he had killed within himself. It is this humanity that he is forced to resurrect. In truth, his murdering and his conversion (what some critics call a journey to self-knowledge) are not clearly linked in the novel, because Bigger is never allowed to focus on the brutality of his crimes or on the horror of his acts. He sees himself as other men see him, but he does not ever resee his smothering of Mary, his cutting off of her head, his bludgeoning of Bessie. It is not in Wright's formulated ideology of the book for Bigger to relive these things. But if we study the evolution of Bigger's sense of humanity, his metamorphosis, without Wright's direction, without Max's speeches, it becomes clear that when Bigger says, "What I killed for must've been good! . . . I know how it sounds. But I'm all right. I feel all right when I look at it that way. . . ." (501; the second ellipsis is original to the text), we have an indication that Wright knows how unacceptable this statement is. Bigger's words alienate Max, the reader, and to some degree the author himself.

In the end, Wright has Bigger deny the responsibility for his crime by calling the crime "good"; a wrong—we all know—does not make a right. The Bigger who has been morally converted is still visible when he tells Max, "[T]hinking's made me scared a little" (495), and we sense that he has come to admit fear, a thing that before he simply struck out against or blotted out. We also begin to see that he genuinely felt some regret for his crimes; his saying "I didn't mean to do what I did" and "But really I never wanted to hurt nobody" might be understood as equivalent to "I'm sorry for what I did; I regret killing Mary and Bessie. If I had it to do over again, I wouldn't." But Bigger doesn't mean this, finally; he justifies his crimes, steels himself against the pain of recognition. Wright describes him as grabbing the steel bars of his cell door after admitting, "But I ain't hard, Mr. Max. I ain't hard even a little bit. . . . But . . . I—I won't be crying none when they take me to that chair. But I'll b-b-be feeling inside of me like I was crying. . . . I'll be feeling and thinking that they didn't see me and I didn't see them" (496; ellipses original to the text, but the first contains an ellipsis not in the text). Had the novel ended here, this would have been an acceptable conclusion, a place from which to teach—for it is here that the novel can be used to heal division, to point to the responsibilities of life, to the role of the individual in a community of people whether alike or assorted. It is here, too, that the novel can be used to illustrate the need for self-examination and truth. Moreover, the novel can allow (does allow) teachers to speak persuasively to students about a world that need not remain tortured and divided by race, class, and gender.

The future of the students in our courses has never been in question; their fate, their paths have never been the same as Bigger's. What students have in common with Bigger is the experience of being the other in America. Whether black, white, Asian, or Native American, students at every level know how they are different, and those new to this country learn it soon enough. *Native Son* may not provide them all with a fresh vision of unity, but at least it need not teach them the absolute fatalism and despair that attend Bigger's life. It need not imply that we teachers and critics value this vision (by continuing to teach the book as ever) even while we condemn the system that perpetuates the conditions that give rise to fictional or living Biggers.

Prophetically or problematically, Wright left us looking at Bigger through the steel bars of his prison cell. He is smiling a "faint, wry, bitter smile." The door he hears clang shut is the "ring of steel against steel" (502). I believe that if teachers continue to teach *Native Son* without emphasizing Wright's failure to allow Bigger to accept the painful responsibility of his acts, those of us who teach the book may as well accept that final image of Bigger as one of ourselves—imprisoned by the bitter criticisms of this text, by the promulgated and generalized assumptions about teaching and reading this text, and by the unchallenged conditions of our racist society that this text does allow us to see and begin to deconstruct in our classrooms. Should we fail to teach *Native Son* as a lesson in truth, we will remain locked in steel cages of convention and repetition, and our students will never learn to stand commitedly with "the side that feels life most, the side with the most humanity" (500).

Max, Media, and Mimesis:
Bigger's Representation in *Native Son*

Michael Bérubé

My reading of *Native Son* rests largely on Bigger's "representation" by the International Labor Defense attorney Boris Max and State's Attorney David A. (DA) Buckley. My argument, in brief, is that *Native Son* is about African American representation in the legal and in the mimetic sense, and that the novel enacts its concerns with representation partly by representing itself in its own narrative machinery. I start by focusing on Max's defense, because many readers, over the last fifty years, have taken it to be the summation of the novel, almost as if Max is representing Richard Wright as well as Bigger Thomas.[1] In the past, I've asked students to find flaws in Max's defense. In response, some students call attention to the bizarrely Foucauldian passage in which Max speaks of Bigger's possible imprisonment:

> It will at least indicate that we *see* and *know*! . . . To send him to prison would be more than an act of mercy. You would be for the first time conferring *life* upon him. He would be brought for the first time within the orbit of our civilization. He would have an identity, even though it be but a number. . . . Sending him to prison would be the first recognition of his personality he has ever had.
> (471)

Other students, echoing a few of the novel's first reviewers,[2] object to the passage in which Max construes Bigger as a synecdoche for all of black America: "Multiply Bigger Thomas twelve million times, allowing for environmental and temperamental variations, and for those Negroes who are completely under the influence of the church, and you have the psychology of the Negro people" (463).

It's worth noting that Max's insistence on Bigger as symbol, like his insinuation that Bigger needs to be brought within the ambit of "civilization," is uncomfortably similar to the rhetorical strategies employed by the prosecution.[3] But in the recent past I have begun class discussion otherwise, by pointing out that Max's plea of guilty in Bigger's case is as questionable a legal strategy as that employed by the defense in Mike Tyson's 1992 rape trial. The Tyson-Bigger intertext is, of course, both rich and volatile. Just as Tyson's defense team argued that their client was so notoriously unstable and dangerous, so Bigger-like, that no prudent woman would meet him alone at midnight, so too does Max start from the premise that Bigger must be established as pathological. Though Max adopts this line of defense in order to argue that Bigger is but a symptom of a larger national pathology, he never challenges the prosecution's charge of rape. As in the Tyson trial, the "defense" explains *why* the bigger bad-nigger acts the way he does instead of attempting to sow the seeds of reasonable doubt in the minds of the jurors. The gender politics of both defense strategies are similar, too, and similarly odious. Where the Tyson team blames the woman, Max ignores Bigger's killing of Bessie.

The classic critique of Max's strategy was formulated by Benjamin Davis Jr. in the *Sunday Worker* of 14 April 1940, where he notes that if Max were truly an ILD lawyer, he would have contested the charge that Bigger raped Mary, would have dealt with the murder of Bessie, and would have entered a plea of not guilty.[4] Davis himself was an African American official in the Communist Party, so his critique is something of a partisan review. But his was the only contemporary review of the novel to take Max's speech seriously for its legal and propositional content, and one of the few reviews to register outrage that Bessie's murder is of no moment to the court—no moment because, as Bigger himself knew, "white people did not really care about Bessie's being killed. . . . He had even heard it said that white people felt it was good when one Negro killed another; it meant that they had one Negro less to contend with" (383). More recent commentators have pointed out that Max's defense "speaks for" Bigger in the manner in which white Americans have long represented blackness to one another. As Robert Stepto puts it, "While transcending the character type in the slave narratives which he first resembles, Max soon takes on the features of a familiar turn-of-the-century type, the 'white moral voice'" ("I Thought" 532).[5] In other words, Max may not be representative of the ILD or the Communist Party, but he may plausibly be said to represent the figure of the sympathetic white man who doesn't quite understand the widespread racial unrest of which he speaks. In this respect I have sometimes thought that Max might be an uncomfortable analogue for my own position in the classroom— even though Bigger's life does not depend on whether I persuade my students that my interpretation is plausible.

State's Attorney Buckley employs a rather different sense of representation. He has no interest in trying to depict Bigger faithfully; his declaration, instead, is that he, Buckley, represents the people. His opening statement makes this point in histrionic fashion. On surveying the courtroom crowd, Buckley cries, "It is not often . . . that a representative of the people finds the masses of the citizens who elected him to office standing literally at his back, waiting for him to enforce the law" (433). Having thus identified their clients, Buckley and Max square off for the right to frame Bigger's representation. *Native Son* begins to re-present itself in astonishingly minute detail, as the novel basically retells its first hundred pages from the perspectives of Buckley, Max, and the court officials who recite "over and over" the charges that Bigger raped and killed both Bessie and Mary (429). One might say, in fact, that the function of the entire legal apparatus in *Native Son* is to retell *Native Son*, for no sooner is Mary's disappearance discovered than Bigger has to listen to people like Britten, the private eye, "tell the story all over again" (240).

Accordingly, the novel's third section is heavily, even obsessively, repetitious. Though Bigger declines to reenact the crime at the Dalton house, for instance, Buckley reenacts it in the courtroom, and he calls to the stand sixty witnesses, including sixteen police officers, fifteen newspapermen, six doctors, five handwriting analysts, five psychiatrists, and four black waitresses. No doubt many readers have had reason to agree with Morris Dickstein that the novel's conclusion amounts to little more than a "curious but inert ideological essay," an "immensely long and disappointing coda" (161). If readers are looking for suspense, horror, and rooftop chases, *Native Son's* trial scene can only be a disappointment.

But in my reading, the point of the trial is precisely to represent the novel. One would think that Buckley's sixty witnesses were sufficient to try the case; but he proceeds to comb through the novel for each of the artifacts relevant to Bigger's crimes.

> Buckley brought forth the knife and purse Bigger had hidden in the garbage pail [on pages 111–12] and informed the Court that the city's dump had been combed for four days to find them. The brick he had used to strike Bessie with was shown; then came the flashlight, the Communist pamphlets, the gun, the blackened earring, the hatchet blade, the signed confession, the kidnap note, Bessie's bloody clothes, the stained pillows and quilts, the trunk, and the empty rum bottle which had been found in the snow near a curb. (441)

The novel's opening pages depict workmen plastering Bigger's neighborhood with a campaign poster for Buckley, a poster that features "one of those faces that looked straight at you when you looked at it and all the while you were walking and turning your head to look at it it kept looking unblinkingly back at you" (12–13). It's safe to say, given the above inventory, that the poster is a "true" representation, that it really works: apparently, Buckley and the Chicago police can see everything Bigger does and can represent it to themselves for their own purposes.[6] In court, having presented their witnesses and represented the novel's data, they then stage what's now called a "dramatic reenactment" of Bigger's attempt to burn Mary's body, using the furnace itself rather than a replica:

> [A] group of twelve workmen brought in the furnace, piece by piece, from the Dalton basement and mounted it upon a giant wooden platform. . . . Buckley had a white girl [!], the size of Mary, crawl inside the furnace "to prove beyond doubt that it could and did hold and burn the ravished body of innocent Mary Dalton; and to show that the poor girl's head could not go in and the sadistic Negro cut it off." (441–42)

Fortunately for Mary's understudy, Buckley does not pursue strict verisimilitude this once.

The state's powers of surveillance are by no means limited to the accumulation of material objects; Buckley, like a hyperrealist novelist, can also make a narrative of his evidence. He claims, disingenuously, that he will be sullied by the very narration of the story: "[L]iterally I shrink from the mere recital of this dastardly crime. I cannot speak of it without feeling somehow contaminated by the mere telling of it" (476–77). Despite his sense of contamination, he proceeds to retell Bigger's story for some seven pages, disclosing along the way that he even knows that Bigger "did not want to work" (477) and had "consented only when his mother informed him that the relief would cut off their supply of food if he did not accept" (478; his mother had complained to Bigger, "even when the relief offers you a job you won't take it till they threaten to cut off your food" [7]).

Wright's immediate point, certainly, has to do with the extent to which residents of Chicago's South Side are living in a police state, where the mental and physical contents of their lives may be dragged into the public sphere and represented by the state for the purpose of incarcerating or killing them. It's quite clear that the conditions of ghetto life, in *Native Son* as in the United States, amount to a form of psychological terrorism. The anger Bigger feels in court is the anger of the captive, "an old feeling that Bessie had often described to him when she had come from long hours of hot toil in the white folks' kitchens, a feeling of being forever commanded by others so much that thinking and feeling for one's self was impossible" (383). It's fitting, therefore, that Buckley be such an omniscient, if unsympathetic, narrator. But then what's odd about the trial in *Native Son* is that Max's representation also performs a kind of psychological surveillance of Bigger, likewise displaying the details of Bigger's interiority to the court. If Max were having Bigger plead innocent, there would be little wrong with this; Max is performing an affirmative task simply in demonstrating to the court that Bigger has an interiority—that he is not, as Buckley would have it, a "half-human black ape" (476), a "black lizard" (476), or a "demented savage" (483). But since Max ultimately pleads for Bigger's imprisonment, there's something deeply unsettling about Max's ability to represent Bigger's innermost thoughts while Bigger remains mute.

In the first section of the novel, for instance, the narrator writes: "To Bigger and his kind white people were not really people; they were a sort of great natural force, like a stormy sky looming overhead, or like a deep swirling river stretching suddenly at one's feet in the dark" (129). Over three hundred pages later, Max knows, as surely as if he had already read *Native Son*, that people such as Bigger "feel that they are facing mountains, floods, seas: forces of nature" (450). As we were told that Bigger "had killed many times before" (119, 277), so does Max know that "he has murdered many times" (466); as we heard that "these two murders were the most meaningful things that had ever happened to him" (277), so does Max know that Mary's murder "was the most meaningful, exciting and stirring thing that had ever happened to him" (461).

It is altogether appropriate that *Native Son* closes with extensive representations of Bigger by the legal representatives of the Communist Party and the state of Illinois. As I suggested above, the entire novel is about African American representation, if we understand "representation" not merely in its legal sense but also as it pertains to media and mimesis. The Chicago press coverage of Bigger, for example, is every bit as obsessively panoptic as Buckley's prosecution of Bigger is, and the novel's second half is nearly as devoted to Chicago news accounts as it is to Bigger's capture and trial. Much of the end of "Flight," the second book, seems narrated simultaneously by Wright and the press; Bigger himself has to read the *Tribune* and *Times* to discover the status of the authorities' search for him, almost as if the novel were providing him with maps pinpointing his (subject) position. In order that Bigger might locate himself more easily, the *Times* employs a graphic representation of Chicago's South Side wherein the "[s]haded portion shows area already covered by police and vigilantes in search for Negro rapist and murderer. White portion shows area yet to be searched" (284). Shortly thereafter, the white area having dwindled in a later edition of the paper, Bigger buys a *Times*, scans the front page, and knows that "he [is] there on that map, in that white spot, standing in a room waiting for them to come" (296).

The press's representations of Bigger, of course, are matter for comment throughout the second half of *Native Son*. Notably, they are also representations of the *Chicago Tribune's* openly racist reporting of the 1938 Robert Nixon case, as Wright indicates in "How Bigger Was Born" (532). More to our present purposes, they represent the words of fictional "authorities" who serve to testify for the state. Consider the "[p]rofessional psychologists at the University of Chicago" who certify that "white women have an unusual fascination for Negro men" (424) or the editor of the *Jackson (Mississippi) Daily Star*, who affirms in the *Tribune* that Bigger is reputed to have "a minor portion of white blood in his veins, a mixture which generally makes for a criminal and intractable nature" (324).[7]

Bigger is understandably overwhelmed by his press coverage. In his brief career as a fugitive, although he notes with some pride that "[t]he papers ought to be full of him now" (256), he is taken aback at how completely white America controls the means of representation and at how his own narrative becomes theirs almost instantaneously. Indeed, when he realizes how quickly the press can re-present scenes he has just witnessed, he begins to despair:

> That the image of Mr. and Mrs. Dalton which he had seen but two hours ago should be seen again so soon [in the paper] made him feel that this whole vague white world which could do things this quickly was more than a match for him, that soon it would track him down and have it out with him. . . . There would be a thousand white policemen on the South Side searching for him or any black man who looked like him.   (258)

In this Bigger could not be more correct: because the police and the papers own the means of representation, they not only can keep him under constant media surveillance but also can make of him a "representative" African American criminal as well.

Yet the media have always been Bigger's primary influence, whether he's tracking the police and press tracking him or whether he's watching the movie *Trader Horn* with its "African scene" of "naked black men and women whirling in wild dances and . . . drums beating" (36). He decides to ditch Bessie because "[h]e had read of how men had been caught because of women" (162); he writes a ransom note, as Max says later, because he "got the idea from the newspapers" (337); and when he thinks he has "his destiny in his grasp," he feels that "he [is] moving toward that sense of fulness he . . . so often but inadequately felt in magazines and movies" (170). If *Native Son* is a novel about the representation of African Americans, it is also about Bigger's interpellation by mass media—and in this respect, too, Wright suggests that Bigger is representative of dispossessed African American youth.[8]

It's possible to criticize the politics of Wright's insistent emphasis on representation, as Ralph Ellison did when he remarked that "in *Native Son* Wright began with the ideological proposition that what whites think of the Negro's reality is more important than what Negroes themselves knew it to be" ("Blues" 114). But amidst our media-saturated postmodern condition, in which the representation of "race" is also its construction, I think we have some reason to reply that whites still control most of the dominant means of media representation in the United States and that usually they construct blackness on principles very different from those which "Negroes themselves" know. On these grounds we might suggest that *Native Son* is less concerned with Bigger's representativeness than with Bigger's multiple representations, and what these tell us about the processes by which blackness is constructed and consumed. And because *Native Son* itself is, after all, one of the important vehicles by which blackness has been represented to Americans of all ethnicities and races, it may be of some use to teach the novel alongside Trey Ellis's 1988 novel *Platitudes*, a text much more self-consciously concerned with the intersections among mass media, American literature, and the multiple identities of African Americans. (And it's relevant here that *Platitudes* launches itself by signifying on *Native Son*'s opening scene.)[9] Finally, since Wright's novel has been so acclaimed for so long, it's also worth asking how its reception made Wright the literary representative of his "race" and how influential white critics, from Fisher (1940) to Irving Howe (1963: "Black Boys"), attempted to install him as *the* representative African American writer. Asking this question involves assessing the myriad social meanings of *Native Son*'s entry into the American canon, and it involves inviting students to consider how American canons—of the 1940s and 1990s—have represented blackness and its relation to America.

NOTES

[1]As James Miller has pointedly written, however, "Max does not speak for Bigger Thomas, nor does he speak for Richard Wright. He attempts to *represent* Bigger, in both a legal and linguistic sense, and fails" (505).

[2]Peter Monro Jack, writing in the *New York Times Book Review*, concluded that "Mr. Wright does spoil his story at the end by insisting on Bigger's fate as representative of the whole Negro race and by making Bigger himself say so" (20). Benjamin Davis Jr. likewise warned that "one of the serious weaknesses of the book, particularly in the third part, is that the author overwrites Bigger into a symbol of the whole Negro people, a native son to the Negro people" (Reilly, *Richard Wright* 71). Patronizing white readers, however, were likely to praise Bigger for his representativity, as did Dorothy Canfield Fisher, whose introduction to the novel spoke of it as if Bigger and Wright, together, represented not only all African Americans but also every manner of psychologically disturbed animal. *Native Son*, she wrote, is "the first report in fiction we have had from those . . . whose behavior-patterns give evidence of the same bewildered, senseless tangle of abnormal nerve-reactions studied in animals by psychologists in laboratory experiments" (x).

[3]Likewise, both attorneys figure the South Side as a jungle: where Max speaks of Bigger in the "wild forest of our great cities, amid the rank and choking vegetation of slums" (456), Buckley calls for the judge "to tell [the people] that jungle law does not prevail in this city" (483). Needless to say, the jungle imagery tends to work better for Buckley. Reilly notes a correspondence between Buckley's accounts and the narrative voice of the novel: "The racist versions of Bigger's story bear crucial resemblance to the summary statements of his psychology related early in the novel, out of intimate knowledge, by the presiding narrative voice" ("Giving" 52).

[4]Davis's summary of Max's performance is severe: "He argues that Bigger, and by implication the whole Negro mass, should be held in jail to protect 'white daughters' though capitalism is plainly the guilty criminal which threatens poor white womanhood as well as Negro. . . . From Max's whole conduct the first business of the Communist Party or of the I.L.D. would have been to chuck him out of the case" (Reilly, *Richard Wright* 75).

[5]Keneth Kinnamon makes a similar argument with regard to Wright's negotiations with his editor, Edward Aswell, suggesting that Aswell "may even be regarded as standing in relation to Wright as Max stands in relation to Bigger: sympathetic, loyal, analytical, understanding to a point, but not quite ready to accept the full and uncut expression of a sensibility so radically different from his own" (Introduction 16). On a related note, Kinnamon also proposes that Fisher's introduction to *Native Son* is "a latter-day example of the process of white authentication which Robert Stepto has shown to be so characteristic a feature of slave narratives" (17).

[6]Buckley astonishes Bigger when he reveals that he knows about the planned robbery of Blum's store; Buckley also knows that Bigger and his friend Jack masturbated in the Regal Theatre (354).

[7]My students had special difficulty with the fictional *Tribune* report of the inquest (322–24), considering it to be an overdrawn and cartoonish parody of the paper. Unfortunately for Robert Nixon, my students, and the staff of the *Tribune*, Wright's version is all too faithful to its original. For discussion of the Nixon case (and damning citations of the article on which Wright drew), see Kinnamon, *Native Son* 122–24; Kinnamon, Introduction 5–6.

[8]For more on Wright's use of media, see John Williams ("Use").

[9]Earle Tyner, the protagonist of a novel called *Platitudes* (authored by Dewayne Wellington, a fictional writer in Ellis's novel *Platitudes*), is, like Bigger, rudely awakened by the ringing of an alarm clock. The difference is that Earle lives not on Chicago's South Side but on New York's Upper West Side, where, as a young black urban professional-to-be, he attends an elite private high school and dreams of teaching computer science at "Caltech or M.I.T. or someplace like that" (3).

Doing the (W)Right Thing:
Approaching Wright and Lee

Gary Storhoff

I have taught *Native Son* in a variety of literature classes, to students from extraordinarily wide ranges of background, age, and socioeconomic status. I am generally fascinated by the readiness of students to reenvision the novel with reference to their own lives. In every class, students are eager to tell their reconstruction of the narrative, for Wright leads (as does no other author) readers to tell their own stories, their own struggles with racial and class bias. Their compulsion to narrate their own tales certainly has to do with Wright's decision to disallow readers the consolation of easy sympathy for Bigger, Wright's refusal to write a book "which even bankers' daughters could read and weep over and feel good about" (531). There are no facile explanations for Bigger—as his mother, Jan, and finally Max discover. Students, given their strongly ambivalent emotional response to Bigger, are forced to judge his story in literal or referential terms, contextualizing it within the framework of their observed social roles. Wright's reader is not so much an "implied" reader as an implicated one.

In my classes I attempt to demonstrate Wright's artistic method of breaking down boundaries between fiction and the socially constructed experience that my students often describe as "the real world." It is, of course, important to avoid the condescending view that *Native Son* is simply a sociological treatise—an assumption that David Bradley decries in his moving, personal response to the novel; nevertheless, to underestimate Wright's ability to "draw readers in," to induce readers to carry Wright's views into their own world, is to ignore Wright's controlling moral purpose in the novel.

One passage that has provoked an especially hot exchange among students occurs early in the novel, when Bigger is going to the Dalton house to be interviewed for the job. He debates whether he should carry his knife and gun and finally decides to go armed: "Then he thought of a good reason why he should take [a gun]; in order to get to the Dalton place, he had to go through a white neighborhood. He had not heard of any Negroes being molested recently, but he felt that it was always possible" (48). Events in Bensonhurst and Howard Beach make Bigger's anxiety sound like current headlines.[1] Yet white suburban students are often surprised by Wright's statement, since they assume their neighborhoods are safe; it is the notorious sections of neighboring cities that are off limits. One African American student, living in an inner city in southwestern Connecticut, told us that he is stopped by police virtually every time he drives through one of the more exclusive suburban towns in Fairfield County; that he is pulled over, sometimes searched, and generally treated with hostility and suspicion. Another student, coincidentally a policeman from that same town, admitted that he stopped "suspicious outsiders," not (of course) because he was racist but because it was his job to serve and protect the residents. The argument between the two was predictable, but it clarified in many ways the central issue of *Native Son*: the enforcement of restricted space.

Students inevitably confront the boundaries that racism throws before us, and Wright focuses on those boundaries. Space in the novel, whether it is the suffocating enclosure of Bigger's apartment or the politically devised incarceration represented by the grid of Chicago's streets, ironically reverses the traditionally American sense of liberty inherent in American geography. As Houston A. Baker writes, "Afro-America was a PLACE *assigned* rather than discovered" ("Richard Wright" 92; see also Harris). Baker's insight clarifies not only the spatial but also the moral dimensions of the novel. As Bigger leaves his house to go to the job interview, he almost immediately confronts a "high, black, iron picket fence"—an objective correlative for his "constricted [feeling] inside" (49). The fence is one of many images in the novel that tell him he has reached, with incredible abruptness, the limits of his journey and that sustain the novel's metaphorical patterns of enclosure. Bigger's wish to go beyond his boundaries, to "[trespass] into territory where the full wrath of an alien white world would be turned loose upon [him]" (14), draws self-observations from the students: To what extent are boundaries enforced in the social world the reader inhabits? To what extent do we participate in upholding those boundaries?

Students notice the profusion of wall and boundary imagery, and they are intuitively aware of space as an assigned commodity in the novel. They are also aware of Bigger's subordination in a system where space assignments are a life-and-death matter. The issue of occupying a place is complicated by the novel's white characters. When Wright reveals that Mr. Dalton owns the company that leases Mrs. Thomas her apartment, we realize that whatever the dimensions of his freedom, he is not limited in space; not only can he move freely about in Chicago, but he also owns the rat-infested slum the Thomases ironically perceive as theirs. Mr. Dalton's freedom of movement is matched by Jan's and Mary's, since they can with impunity invade Bigger's space when they go for a lunch on the South Side. During the lunch, place becomes a central subject of discussion: "We want to go to a *real* place," Mary tells him (78), complaining of her exclusion from Bigger's home: "You know, Bigger, I've long wanted to go into those houses . . . and just *see* how your people live. You know what I mean? I've been to England, France and Mexico, but I don't know how people live ten blocks from me. . . . I just want to *see*" (79). Disguised in Mary's speech is the discourse of space: her ignorance of the narrow boundaries of Bigger's world, contrasted with the expansiveness of her world.

The anguish of bumping up against a close limitation is increased when one cannot relate the experience of constriction. Kathleen Gallagher has written of how desperately Bigger wants someone to listen to him (307), and many other critics have written extensively about the problematics of Wright's manipulation of point of view (see esp. Ellison, "Blues"; J. A. Miller; Stepto, "I Thought";

Tremaine). But Bigger's forced inarticulateness is an assumption that begins the critical dialogue between Jan, Mary, and Bigger—and in fact is a contributing cause of Mary's killing. Students seldom investigate closely enough the specific causes of Mary's death. She dies because Bigger's freedom to speak, to tell his own story of the fateful evening with Jan and Mary, is denied him, largely because of the forbidden territory he finds himself suddenly inhabiting—Mary's bedroom. If he were to speak, he would only convict himself, for the simple reason that he occupies a prohibited space. (Ironically, he is later described as a rapist anyway by the district attorney.) That Mrs. Dalton's unwitting suppression of Bigger's voice leads to Mary's death is conveyed primarily through Wright's structuring of space in the bedroom scene. Mrs. Dalton blocks Bigger's way to the door, as if she were yet another imposing wall: "A white blur was standing by the door, silent, ghostlike. It filled his eyes and gripped his body. It was Mrs. Dalton. He wanted to knock her out of his way and bolt from the room" (97). But blind, frail Mrs. Dalton is an immovable obstacle for Bigger. Because her presence at the open door—representing both a silencing and a physical entrapment—forces Bigger to stifle Mary's speech, Wright implies that Mrs. Dalton, despite her "innocent" liberalism, thereby becomes complicit in the killing of her daughter. In this novel, no one, including a politically naive liberal, is innocent.

To broaden the context of *Native Son*, I teach *Do the Right Thing* as a complement in the classes that follow. Like Wright, Spike Lee deconstructs the fictive boundaries of his film, so that its world intrudes into our "real" one. I assign the film to be viewed before class discussion, and I present brief scenes from the film to provoke discussion. I also put on reserve Spike Lee's companion journal, which includes his notes and comments on his formal intentions.

It is easy for us to see, without necessarily positing an influence, that Wright's novelistic concerns anticipate Lee's filmic themes. The issue of assigned space is at the heart of Lee's film also and is enunciated in the pivotal scene. The character Buggin' Out, disgruntled over the price of Sal's pizza and his stinginess with cheese, spitefully demands that "black faces" be hung on Sal's Wall of Fame, which is covered with pictures of Italian American celebrities in the entertainment industry. (Could this be Lee's own statement about his difficulties with Hollywood producers?) The film's frame shows on the same wall the truncated, shadowed reflection of Sal's store window: SAUSA [SAUSAGE]. The implication of a correspondence between the United States and South African apartheid might too easily be dismissed by the viewer as Lee's polemical bombast, were it not for Lee's subtlety throughout the film in arguing that certain spaces are indeed proscribed for African Americans.

In Sal's Famous, the Wall of Fame is symbolic of black exclusion from other, much more significant fields of activity. In the restaurant itself, Sal makes clear that Mookie must never go behind the counter, where the cash register is located; for Mookie, the space behind the counter (controlled by whites) is a synecdoche for his absence from the marketplace. That Mookie is more or less free to roam the entire community—except behind the counter—emphasizes Lee's point of proscribed spaces and recalls Wright's message.

The motif of proscribed spaces is reiterated constantly in the film, most notably in the Corner Men, who are literally defined by their occupied space; significantly, it is they who explicitly comment on the problem of economic opportunity (though Lee's treatment of them is tinged with irony). Their paralysis is indeed a "waste," as the cruising cops mutter to each other, but surely the Corner Men's inactivity is at least partly a consequence of an entire lifetime of confronting barriers. In contrast with the characters who have little freedom of movement are the characters who can invade Bed-Stuy at will. The owner of the antique Cadillac, for example, whose rage over his doused car brings the police, may be an improbable intruder in Bed-Stuy, but his presence underscores an unreflective freedom that none of the black characters can assume. The yuppy in the brownstone and the Korean grocers also express by their presence an essentially colonialist attitude toward the appropriation and control of privatized spaces. Sal, of course, is the most significant intruder. However positively students respond to his friendliness and his work ethic, they all see that his business is successful mainly because it is a monopoly that he could not have enjoyed in an Italian American neighborhood.

Once students recognize the similarity between Wright's and Lee's thematic designs, I suggest further connections, especially in Lee's commentary on communicative events. Lee's characters, like those in *Native Son*, do not listen to one another, and Lee uses the radio motif to underscore their communication failure. For example, at the film's beginning, Pino tries to order Vito to sweep the street, but Vito wears earphones and remains oblivious until badgered into hearing. Vito does not accept his subservient role. More significant, Love Daddy uses the medium of radio to promote love, harmony, and tolerance; but though his audience hears him and his music, he and his music are only a distraction, and no one really accepts and acts on his messages. The most obvious development of the radio motif is, of course, Radio Raheem, who continuously plays "Fight the Power" on his boom box. At some level, this song must articulate for Raheem his sense of exclusion and his political rage. Even so, Raheem is silent about the song's political lyrics and tells Buggin' Out that he plays this music simply because he doesn't really like anything else. Raheem, who introduces himself with "Peace, y'all," apparently isn't listening to his own deafening sounds. If, as James Miller suggests, *Native Son* develops the pattern of call and response through Bigger's dealings with the black community (502), Lee devises that pattern only to demonstrate its failure: characters listen to the call inadequately and respond inadequately.

Perhaps the film's central speaker is Mookie. His Bigger-like action at the film's end—inciting the riot that destroys Sal's Famous—expresses a message that many cannot listen to. Much like Wright's Bigger, Lee's Mookie acts at a critical moment because he cannot speak. Ironically, Mookie's message has been unheard, not only by the film's characters, but also by the film's critics, who have tended to oversimplify Mookie's action (seeing it as an example of "black racism"). But students appreciate the full political dimensions of Lee's character when they study the journal that was published as a companion text to the film. When the germ idea of the film first occurred to Lee (on 25 December 1987), Mookie was to represent black militancy. Lee writes:

> The character I play in *Do the Right Thing* is from the Malcolm X school of thought: "An eye for an eye." . . . [He] sees a great injustice take place and starts the riot. He turns a garbage can upside down, emptying the trash in the street. Then he goes up to the pizza parlor screaming, "An eye for an eye, Howard Beach," and hurls the garbage can.   (34)

The second time Lee envisions the final scene, he drops the "eye for an eye" line, lessening Mookie's character as a political ideologue but still casting him as the film's revolutionary: "I pick up the garbage can, dump the garbage in the street, and scream 'Howard Beach'" (41). Finally, as Lee prepares to write the second draft of the script (and shortly before the shooting begins), his journal notation shows that Mookie has evolved almost completely away from racial militancy and toward political subtlety: "One of the problems of the ending of the film as it stands is that Mookie is too impartial when the riot breaks out. He has to be on Radio Raheem's side from the beginning, even if he doesn't get physically involved" (78–79). Thus, following Lee's own commentary, one must see Mookie's decision to throw the garbage can as a problematic response to a desperate political situation.

Lee's journal notations and a close examination of the final scenes reveal the dramatic complexity of Mookie's situation. As Mookie stands with Sal and Sal's two sons "defenseless" (247), the crowd, enraged that Raheem is dead, advances threateningly toward the four, the people shouting their rage not only for Raheem but also for all the other blacks killed because of social brutality—Michael Stewart, Yvonne Smallwood, Eleanor Bumpurs, the victims of the Howard Beach incident. Mookie exchanges a look for several seconds with Sal, then slowly walks away, to be replaced by Da Mayor, who urges the crowd not to harm the three Italian Americans: "If we don't stop this now, we'll all regret it. Sal and his two boys had nothing to do with what the police did" (248). Sal looks at the crowd and says, "Ya do what ya gotta do"—referring, presumably, not to the crowd's compulsion to strike back but to his monopoly in Bed-Stuy and the competition he would face if he moved his pizzeria to his own neighborhood in Bensonhurst. At that point the camera cuts to Mookie's anguished expression. Mookie slowly rubs his face with both hands, then calculatedly walks to the garbage can, slowly and deliberately removes the plastic trash liner, shouts "Hate!," and throws the can through Sal's window.

Do the Right Thing subtly depicts the ramifications of Mookie's gesture—an encoded message that students appreciate because of their own experiences of racial divisiveness. On the one hand, Mookie has witnessed the injustice of Sal's violence against Raheem and the police brutality, he is on Raheem's side, and he has been warned earlier in the film by Buggin' Out to "stay black." On the other hand, he sees the pointlessness of attacking Sal and his two sons for the crime committed by the police—though he also sees the ineffectuality of Da Mayor's plea for nonviolence. No one listens to Da Mayor. Mookie is suddenly positioned in the film to make the same choice the police made (when they killed Raheem) and Sal made (when he refused to put black faces on his Wall of Fame): he must choose between the value of private property and human life. He chooses in favor of Sal and his sons; by throwing the garbage can he shifts the attention of the crowd from the Italians to the Italians' pizzeria. It is Mookie who triggers the riot, but only to deflect the mob from harming Sal—with whom his relationship has been difficult, to say the least. Mookie's message of the thrown garbage can is simple, though largely unheard by either Sal or the audience: human life, white and black, is far more important than property. Mookie does "the right thing."

In this scene, Lee forces my students to confront the multiplicity of meanings in language. Mookie shouts "Hate!" as he runs toward the building, but the word is ambiguous: Who hates? Hate what? It does not necessarily mean that Mookie hates Sal or whites in general; the word could as easily apply to the police or to Pino, the film's figuration of hatred. This signifier could point also to the entirety of social conditions that brought about Mookie's act in the first place—the social construction of race and ethnicity that leads to the creation of boundaries. Neither watching nor participating in the firing of the pizzeria, Mookie sits on the curb (significantly) with his sister Jade (whose name expresses a nonracial sense of hope). Earlier in the film, Jade advocated community activism—an alternative form of combatting racism that Mookie may be willing to consider now. As Sal's Famous burns, Pino, Vito, and Sal stand with Da Mayor, safe from the mob; but, ironically, they stand behind a black iron gate that Da Mayor snaps shut. Now behind yet another barrier, they must experience the same sense of restrictiveness that has defined Mookie's entire life.

Both Mookie and Bigger are silent at critical moments of their lives, but they transcend their forced silence with messages that are intended to be listened to (not merely heard) by a wider audience. Both Wright and Lee focus not only on the silencing of the oppressed but also on the unwillingness of others to listen—and on how this loss of communication affects the minute particulars of our lives. In both *Native Son* and *Do the Right Thing*, the texture of daily life is described with a meticulous attention to contingent experience—to matters of space assignment, to street names, speech, action—that leads us to a greater political, social, and moral alertness about the world before our eyes. Wright and Lee show us that the explosive, dramatic events of our world (the sensational murders, the race riots) are consequent of minor adjustments made every day, in the spaces we inhabit, in the words we say or do not say, in messages we accept or reject.

NOTE

[1]Spike Lee makes several allusions to controversial New York racial incidents in which African Americans were killed. In 1986, Michael Griffith was killed by a car in Howard Beach while being chased by a white gang. In 1989, Yusef Hawkins was shot by a white gang in Bensonhurst. Michael Stewart, Yvonne Smallwood, and Eleanor Bumpurs were all killed while in police custody.

CONTRIBUTORS AND SURVEY PARTICIPANTS

Michael Bérubé, *University of Illinois, Urbana*
SDiane A. Bogus, *De Anza College*
Melba Joyce Boyd, *Wayne State University*
Robert J. Butler, *Canisius College*
Hazel Carby, *Yale University*
Leonard Cassuto, *Fordham University, Lincoln Center*
Angelo Costanzo, *Shippensburg University*
Robert Felgar, *Jacksonville State University*
Donald B. Gibson, *Rutgers University, New Brunswick*
Maryemma Graham, *Northeastern University*
Farah Jasmine Griffin, *University of Pennsylvania*
Yoshinobu Hakutani, *Kent State University, Kent*
James C. Hall, *University of Illinois, Chicago*
Angela Y. Hamilton, *State University of New York, Oswego*
Joyce A. Joyce, *Chicago State University*
James R. Payne, *New Mexico State University, Las Cruces*
Erskine Peters, *University of Notre Dame*
Laura L. Quinn, *Allegheny College*
Ann Rayson, *University of Hawaii, Manoa*
Mariann Russell, *Sacred Heart University*
Wilfred D. Samuels, *University of Utah*
Martha Satz, *Southern Methodist University*
Klaus Schmidt, *Johannes Gutenberg–Universität Mainz*
Scott Slovic, *Southwest Texas State University*
Virginia Whatley Smith, *University of Alabama, Birmingham*
Gary Storhoff, *University of Connecticut, Stamford*
Jerry W. Ward Jr., *Tougaloo College*
Nagueyalti Warren, *Emory University*
Garrett H. White, *Rutgers University, New Brunswick*

WORKS CITED

Aaron, Daniel. *Writers on the Left: Episodes in American Literary Communism*. New York: Columbia UP, 1992.

Abcarian, Richard. *Richard Wright's* Native Son: *A Critical Handbook*. Belmont: Wadsworth, 1970.

Algren, Nelson. "Remembering Richard Wright." *Nation* 28 Jan. 1961: 85.

Awkward, Michael. "Negotiations of Power: White Critics, Black Texts, and the Self-Referential Impulse." *American Literary History* 2 (1990): 581–606.

Baker, Houston A., Jr. *Blues, Ideology, and Afro-American Literature: A Vernacular Theory*. Chicago: U of Chicago P, 1984.

———. "Richard Wright and the Dynamics of Place in Afro-American Literature." Kinnamon, *New Essays* 85–116.

———, ed. *Twentieth Century Interpretations of* Native Son: *A Collection of Critical Essays*. Englewood Cliffs: Prentice, 1972.

———. *Workings of the Spirit: The Poetics of Afro-American Women's Writing*. Chicago: U of Chicago P, 1991.

Bakish, David. *Richard Wright*. New York: Ungar, 1973.

Baldwin, James. "Alas, Poor Richard." *Nobody Knows My Name: More Notes of a Native Son*. New York: Dial, 1961. 181–215.

———. "Everybody's Protest Novel." Baldwin, *Notes* 13–23.

———. "Many Thousands Gone." Baldwin, *Notes* 24–45.

———. *Notes of a Native Son*. Boston: Beacon, 1955.

Bates, Karen Grisby. "'They've Gotta Have Us': Hollywood's Black Directors." *New York Times Magazine* 14 July 1991: 15+.

Bell, Bernard W. *The Afro-American Novel and Its Tradition*. Amherst: U of Massachusetts P, 1987.

Blassingame, John. *The Slave Community*. New York: Oxford UP, 1972.

Bloom, Harold, ed. *Major Literary Characters: Bigger Thomas*. New York: Chelsea, 1990.

———. *Richard Wright*. New York: Chelsea, 1987.

———. *Richard Wright's* Native Son. New York: Chelsea, 1988.

Bone, Robert A. *The Negro Novel in America*. New Haven: Yale UP, 1958.

———. *Richard Wright*. Minneapolis: U of Minnesota P, 1969.

Bradley, David. "On Rereading *Native Son*." *New York Times* 7 Dec. 1986: 68–79.

Brasmer, William. "Paul Green." Brasmer and Consolo 71–72.

Brasmer, William, and Dominick Consolo. *Black Drama: An Anthology*. Columbus: Merrill, 1970.

Brignano, Russell. *Richard Wright: An Introduction to the Man and His Work*. Pittsburgh: U of Pittsburgh P, 1970.

Bühler, Karl. *Sprachtheorie*. 1934. Stuttgart: Fischer, 1965.

Butler, Robert. Native Son: *The Emergence of a New Black Hero*. Boston: Twayne, 1991.

Campbell, Ouida. "Bigger Is Reborn." *Carolina Magazine* Oct. 1940: 21–23.

Cappetti, Carla. *Writing Chicago: Modernism, Ethnography, and the Novel*. New York: Columbia UP, 1993.

Carby, Hazel V. "Ideologies of Black Folk: The Historical Novel of Slavery." *Slavery and the Literary Imagination*. Ed. Deborah E. McDowell and Arnold Rampersad. Baltimore: Johns Hopkins UP, 1989. 125–43.

Carter, Dan T. *Scottsboro: A Tragedy of the American South*. Baton Rouge: Louisiana State UP, 1969.

Cleaver, Eldridge. "Convalescence." Cleaver, *Soul* 191–204.

———. "Primeval Mitosis." Cleaver, *Soul* 176–90.

———. *Soul on Ice*. New York: McGraw, 1968.

Cohn, David L. "Review of *Native Son*." Wright and Fabre 57–62. Rpt. of "The Negro Novel: Richard Wright." *Atlantic Monthly* May 1940: 659–61.

Cooke, Michael G. *Afro-American Literature in the Twentieth Century: The Achievement of Intimacy*. New Haven: Yale UP, 1984.

Crew, Spencer R. *Field to Factory: Afro-American Migration, 1915–1940*. Washington: Smithsonian, 1987.

Crossman, Richard H. S., ed. *The God That Failed*. New York: Harper, 1949.

Cruse, Harold. *The Crisis of the Negro Intellectual*. New York: Quill, 1984.

Davis, Benjamin, Jr. Rev. of *Native Son*, by Richard Wright. *Sunday Worker* 14 Apr. 1940, sec. 2: 4+. Rpt. in Reilly, *Richard Wright* 68–76.

Davis, Charles T., and Michel Fabre. *Richard Wright: A Primary Bibliography*. Boston: Hall, 1982.

Davis, Jane. "More Force Than Human: Richard Wright's Female Characters." *Obsidian II* 1 (1968): 68–83.

Deleuze, Gilles, and Felix Guattari. "What Is a Minor Literature?" *Out There: Marginalization and Contemporary Cultures*, 59–70. Ed. Russell Ferguson et al. Cambridge: MIT P, 1990.

Dickstein, Morris. *Gates of Eden: American Culture in the Sixties*. New York: Basic, 1977.

Dixon, Melvin. *Ride Out the Wilderness: Geography and Identity in Afro-American Literature*. Urbana: U of Illinois P, 1987.

Doane, Mary Ann. *The Desire to Desire: The Woman's Film of the 1940's*. Bloomington: Indiana UP, 1987.

Dollard, John. *Caste and Class in a Southern Town*. 3rd ed. Garden City: Doubleday, 1957.

Drake, St. Clair, and Horace R. Cayton. *Black Metropolis: A Study of Negro Life in a Northern City*. 1948. Rev. ed. Chicago: U of Chicago P, 1993.

Du Bois, W. E. B. "A Negro Nation within the Nation." Huggins, *Voices* 384–90.

———. *The Souls of Black Folk*. 1903. New York: Vintage, 1990.

Ellis, Trey. *Platitudes*. New York: Vintage, 1988.

Ellison, Ralph. "Remembering Richard Wright." *Going to the Territory*. New York: Random, 1986. 198–216.

———. "Richard Wright's Blues." Ellison, *Shadow* 77–84.

———. *Shadow and Act*. New York: Random, 1964.

———. "The World and the Jug." Ellison, *Shadow* 107–43.

Fabian, Johannes. *Time and the Other*. New York: Columbia UP, 1983.

Fabre, Michel. "Margaret Walker's Richard Wright: A Wrong Righted or Wright Wronged?" *Mississippi Quarterly* 42 (1989): 429–40.

———. *Richard Wright: Books and Writers*. Jackson: UP of Mississippi, 1990.

———. *The Unfinished Quest of Richard Wright*. Trans. Isabel Barzun. New York: Morrow, 1973.

———. *The World of Richard Wright*. Jackson: UP of Mississippi, 1983.

Fanon, Frantz. *Black Skins, White Masks*. Trans. Charles Lam Markmann. New York: Grove, 1967.

Felgar, Robert. *Richard Wright*. Boston: Twayne, 1980.

Fishburn, Katherine. *Richard Wright's Hero: The Faces of a Rebel-Victim*. Metuchen: Scarecrow, 1977.

Fisher, Dorothy Canfield. Introduction. Wright, *Native Son* [1940]. ix–xi.

Foner, Philip S., and Herbert Shapiro, eds. *American Communism and Black Americans: A Documentary History, 1930–1934*. Philadelphia: Temple UP, 1991.

Foucault, Michel. *Discipline and Punish: The Birth of the Prison*. Trans. Alan Sheridan. New York: Vintage, 1979.

France, Alan W. "Misogyny and Appropriation in Wright's *Native Son*." *Modern Fiction Studies* 34 (1988): 413–23.

Franklin, John Hope. *From Slavery to Freedom: A History of Negro Americans*. New York: Knopf, 1967.

Freedman, Samuel G. "Love and Hate in Black and White." *New York Times* 2 June 1991, sec. 2: 15+.

Gallagher, Kathleen. "Bigger's Great Leap to the Figurative." *CLA Journal* 27 (1984): 293–314.

Gates, Henry Louis, Jr. "'Ethnic and Minority' Studies." *Introduction to Scholarship in Modern Languages and Literatures*. Ed. Joseph Gibaldi. 2nd ed. New York: MLA, 1992. 288–302.

———. *Figures in Black: Words, Signs, and the "Racial" Self*. New York: Oxford UP, 1989.

———. *The Signifying Monkey: A Theory of African-American Literary Criticism*. New York: Oxford UP, 1988.

Gates, Henry Louis, Jr., and K. A. Appiah, eds. *Richard Wright: Critical Perspectives Past and Present*. New York: Amistad, 1993.

Gayle, Addison, Jr. *Richard Wright: Ordeal of a Native Son*. Garden City: Doubleday, 1980.

———. *The Way of the New World: The Black Novel in America*. Garden City: Doubleday, 1976.

Genovese, Eugene. *Roll, Jordon, Roll: The World the Slaves Made*. New York: Random, 1974.

Gibson, Donald B., ed. *Five Black Writers: Essays on Wright, Ellison, Baldwin, Hughes, and LeRoi Jones*. New York: New York UP, 1970.

———. *The Politics of Literary Expression: A Study of Major Black Writers*. Westport: Greenwood, 1981.

———. "Wright's Invisible Native Son." Macksey and Moorer 95–105.

Gilbert, James. *Writers and Partisans: A History of Literary Radicalism in America*. New York: Columbia UP, 1992.

Giroux, Henry. *Teachers as Intellectuals: Toward a Critical Pedagogy of Learning*. Granby: Bergin, 1988.

Gombrich, E. H. *Art and Illusion: A Study in the Psychology of Pictorial Representation*. A. W. Mellon Lectures in the Fine Arts, 1956. 2nd rev. ed. Bollingen Ser. 35. Princeton: Princeton UP, 1961.

Graff, Gerald. "Other Voices, Other Rooms: Organizing and Teaching the Humanities Conflict." *New Literary History* 21 (1990): 917–39.

Green, Paul. *Native Son*. Brasmer and Consolo 73–177.

Green, Paul, and Richard Wright. *Native Son*. *Black Theater U.S.A.* Ed. James V. Hatch. New York: Free, 1974. 393–431.

Grier, William H., and Price M. Cobbs. *Black Rage*. New York: Basic, 1968.

Grossman, James R. *Land of Hope: Chicago, Black Southerners, and the Great Migration*. Chicago: U of Chicago P, 1989.

Hakutani, Yoshinobu, ed. *Critical Essays on Richard Wright*. Boston: Hall, 1982.

———. "*Native Son* and *American Tragedy*: Two Different Interpretations of Crime and Guilt." *Centennial Review* 23 (1978): 208–26.

———. "Richard Wright and American Naturalism." *Zeitschrift für Anglistik und Amerikanistik* 36 (1988); 217–26.

Hansen, Harry. "*Native Son*." Reilly, *Critical Reception* 47–48.

Harris, Trudier. "Native Sons and Foreign Daughters." Kinnamon, *New Essays* 63–84.

Hill, Herbert, Arna Bontemps, and Saunders Redding. "Reflections on Richard Wright: A Symposium on an Exiled Native Son." Gibson, *Five Black Writers* 58–69.

Hirsch, E. D. *Validity in Interpretation*. New Haven: Yale UP, 1967.

Howe, Irving. "Black Boys and Native Sons." *Dissent* 10 (1963): 353–68.

Huggins, Nathan Irvin. *Harlem Renaissance*. New York: Oxford UP, 1972.

———, ed. *Voices from the Harlem Renaissance*. New York: Oxford UP, 1995.

Hughes, Langston. "The Negro Artist and the Racial Mountain." Huggins, *Voices* 305–09.

Hurston, Zora Neale. "How It Feels to Be Colored Me." *I Love Myself When I Am Laughing . . . and Then Again When I Am Looking Mean and Impressive: A Zora Neale Hurston Reader*. Ed. Alice Walker. Old Westbury: Feminist, 1979. 152–55.

———. *Their Eyes Were Watching God*. Philadelphia: Lippincott, 1937.

Jack, Peter Monro. "A Tragic Novel of Negro Life in America." Rev. of *Native Son*, by Richard Wright. *New York Times Book Review* 3 Mar. 1940. 2+.

Jakobson, Roman. *Selected Writings ii*. The Hague: Mouton, 1971.

Johnson, Barbara E. "The Re(a)d and the Black." *Modern Critical Interpretations of Richard Wright's* Native Son. New York: Chelsea, 1988. 115–23.

———. Response to "Canon-Formation, Literary History, and the Afro-American Tradition," by Henry Louis Gates Jr. *Afro-American Literary Study in the 1990s*. Ed. Houston A. Baker Jr. and Patricia Redmond. Chicago: U of Chicago P, 1989. 39–44.

Joyce, Joyce Ann. "The Black Canon: Reconstructing Black American Literary Criticism." *New Literary History* 18 (1986): 335–44.

———. *Richard Wright's Art of Tragedy*. Iowa City: U of Iowa P, 1987.

———. "Style and Meaning in Richard Wright's *Native Son*." *Black American Literature Forum* 16 (1982): 112–15.

Kelley, Robin D. G. *Hammer and Hoe: Alabama Communists during the Great Depression*. Chapel Hill: U of North Carolina P, 1990.

Kent, George. "Richard Wright: Blackness and the Adventure of Western Culture." *Blackness and the Adventure of Western Culture*. Chicago: Third World, 1972. 76–97.

Kinnamon, Keneth. *The Emergence of Richard Wright: A Study in Literature and Society*. Urbana: U of Illinois P, 1972.

———. Introduction. Kinnamon, *New Essays* 1–33.

———. "*Native Son*: The Personal, Social, and Political Background." Hakutani, 120–27.

———, ed. *New Essays on* Native Son. New York: Cambridge UP, 1990.

Kinnamon, Keneth, et al. *A Richard Wright Bibliography: Fifty Years of Criticism and Commentary, 1933–1982*. Westport: Greenwood, 1988.

———. *A Richard Wright Bibliography Supplement*. *The Richard Wright Newsletter* 2.2 (1993): 2–8.

Kostelanetz, Richard. *Politics in the African-American Novel*. New York: Greenwood, 1991.

Kurokawa, Kisho. *Intercultural Architecture: The Philosophy of Symbiosis*. London: Academy, 1991.

Lampert, Anja. "The Character 'Bessie' in Richard Wright's *Native Son*." Unpublished research paper. U of Mainz, Germersheim, 1990.

Lawrence, D. H. *Studies in Classic American Literature*. New York: Viking, 1975.

Lee, Robert A. "Richard Wright's Inside Narratives." *American Fictions: New Readings*. Ed. and introd. Richard Gray. London: Vision; Totowa: Barres, 1983. 200–21.

Lee, Spike. Do the Right Thing: A Spike Lee Joint. New York: Fireside, 1989.

Levine, Lawrence. *Black Culture and Black Consciousness: Afro-American Folk Thought from Slavery to Freedom*. New York: Oxford UP, 1977.

Lynch, Michael F. *Creative Revolt: A Study of Wright, Ellison, and Dostoevsky*. New York: Lang, 1990.

Macke, Eva-Maria. "The Portrayal of the Male-Female Relationship in *Native Son*." Unpublished research paper. U of Mainz, Germersheim, 1991.

Macksey, Richard, and Frank E. Moorer, eds. *Richard Wright: A Collection of Critical Essays*. Englewood Cliffs: Prentice, 1984.

Magistrale, Tony. "From St. Petersburg to Chicago: Wright's Crime and Punishment." *Comparative Literature Studies* 23 (1986): 59–70.

Major, Clarence. "Necessary Distance: Afterthoughts on Becoming a Writer." *Black American Literature Forum* 23 (1989): 218–25.

Mancino, Patrizia. "Richard Wright's *Native Son*: The Role of Violence." Unpublished research paper. U of Mainz, Germersheim, 1991.

Margolies, Edward. *The Art of Richard Wright*. Carbondale: Southern Illinois UP, 1969.

———. "Richard Wright: *Native Son* and Three Kinds of Revolution." *Native Sons: A Critical Study of Twentieth-Century Negro American Authors*. Philadelphia: Lippincott, 1968. 65–86.

McCall, Dan. *The Example of Richard Wright*. New York: Harcourt, 1969.

McCluskey, John, Jr. "'Two Steppin': Richard Wright's Encounter with Blue-Jazz." *American Literature* 55 (1983): 332–44.

McCormick, Kathleen, Gary Waller, and Linda Flower. *Reading Texts*. Lexington: Heath, 1987.

Meier, August, and Elliott Rudwick. *From Plantation to Ghetto*. New York: Hill, 1970.

Miller, Eugene E. *Voice of a Native Son: The Poetics of Richard Wright*. Jackson: UP of Mississippi, 1990.

Miller, James A. "Bigger Thomas's Quest for Voice and Audience in Richard Wright's *Native Son*." *Callaloo* 9 (1986): 501–06.

Mootry, Maria K. "Bitches, Whores, and Woman Haters: Archetypes and Typologies in the Art of Richard Wright." Macksey and Moorer 117–27.

Murphy, James F. *The Proletarian Moment: The Controversy over Leftism in Literature*. Urbana: U of Illinois P, 1991.

Murray, Albert. *The Omni-Americans: Black Experience and American Culture*. New York: Outerbridge, 1970.

Naison, Mark. *Communists in Harlem during the Depression*. New York: Grove, 1984.

Native Son. Dir. Pierre Chenal. Intl. Film Forum, 1950; 1988.

Native Son. Dir. Jerrold Freedman. Cinecom / Diane Silver / American Playhouse, 1986.

Nelles, Simone. "The Portrayal of the Black Community in Richard Wright's *Native Son*." Unpublished research paper. U of Mainz, Germersheim, 1991.

Newlin, Paul. "Why 'Bigger' Lives On: Student Reaction to *Native Son*." Trotman 137–46.

Petry, Ann. *The Street*. 1946. New York: Houghton, 1992.

Poovey, Mary. *Uneven Developments: The Ideological Work of Gender in Mid-Victorian England*. Chicago: U of Chicago P, 1988.

Ray, David, and Robert M. Farnsworth, eds. *Richard Wright: Impressions and Perspectives*. Proc. of Third Annual Inst. for Afro-American Culture, 1971, U of Iowa. Ann Arbor: U of Michigan P, 1973.

Record, Wilson. *The Negro and the American Communist Party*. Chapel Hill: U of North Carolina P, 1951.

Reed, Kenneth T. "*Native Son*: An American *Crime and Punishment*." *Studies in Black Literature* 1 (1970): 33–34.

Reilly, John M. Afterword. 1940. Wright, *Native Son* [1966]. 393–97.

———. "Giving Bigger a Voice: The Politics of Narrative in *Native Son*." Kinnamon, *New Essays* 35–62.

———, ed. *Richard Wright: The Critical Reception*. New York: Franklin, 1978.

Rideout, Walter B. *The Radical Novel in the United States, 1900–1954*. New York: Columbia UP, 1992.

Riggs, Marlon, prod. and dir. *Color Adjustment*. California Newsreel, 1991.

———, prod. and dir. *Ethnic Notions*. California Newsreel, 1987.

Robinson, Cedric. *Black Marxism: The Making of the Black Radical Tradition*. London: Zed, 1983.

Rooney, Ellen. *Seductive Reasoning: Pluralism as the Problematic of Contemporary Literary Theory*. Ithaca: Cornell UP, 1989.

Rosenblatt, Louise M. *Literature as Exploration*. 5th ed. New York: MLA, 1996.

———. *The Reader, the Text, the Poem*. Carbondale: Southern Illinois UP, 1978.

Rubin, Steven J. "Richard Wright and Albert Camus: The Literature of Revolt." *International Fiction Review* 8 (1991): 12–16.

Sartre, Jean-Paul. *Anti-Semite and Jew*. Trans. George J. Becker. 1948. New York: Schocken, 1965.

Schaudt, Carla. "Elements of the Gothic in Richard Wright's *Native Son*." Unpublished research paper. U of Mainz, Germersheim, 1990.

Schuhmacher, Annette. "Richard Wright's *Native Son*: An Analysis of Imagery and Style." Unpublished research paper. U of Mainz, Germersheim, 1991.

Scott, Nathan A., Jr. "The Dark and Haunted Tower of Richard Wright." *Graduate Comment* 7 (1965): 93–99.

Silverman, Kaja. *The Acoustic Mirror: The Female Voice in Psychoanalysis and Cinema*. Bloomington: Indiana UP, 1988.

Smith, Lillian. *Killers of the Dream*. New York: Anchor, 1963.

Smith, Valerie. "Alienation and Creativity in *Native Son*." V. Smith, *Self-Discovery* 65–87.

———. *Self-Discovery and Authority in Afro-American Narrative*. Cambridge: Harvard UP, 1987.

Snead, James A. "Repetition as a Figure of Black Culture." *Black Literature and Literary Theory*. Ed. Henry Louis Gates Jr. New York: Methuen, 1984. 59–79.

Stepto, Robert B. *From behind the Veil: A Study of Afro-American Narrative*. Urbana: U of Illinois P, 1979.

———. "I Thought I Knew These People: Richard Wright and the Afro-American Literary Tradition." *Massachusetts Review* 18 (1977): 525–41.

Stimpson, Catharine R. "Black Culture/White Teacher." *Where the Meanings Are: Feminism and Cultural Spaces*. New York: Routledge, 1988. 1–10.

Tanner, Laura E. "Narrative Presence in *Native Son*." Bloom, 127–42.

Tate, Beverly Daniel. "Talking about Race, Learning about Racism: The Application of Racial Identity Development Theory in the Classroom." *Harvard Educational Review* 62.1 (1992): 1–24.

Tremaine, Louis. "The Dissociated Sensibility of Bigger Thomas in Wright's *Native Son*." *Studies in American Fiction* 14 (1986): 63–76.

Trotman, C. James, ed. *Richard Wright: Myths and Realities*. New York: Garland, 1988.

Walker, Margaret. *Richard Wright: Daemonic Genius*. New York: Warner, 1988.

Wallace, Michelle. *Black Macho and the Myth of the Superwoman*. New York: Dial, 1979.

Warren, Nagueyalti. "Black Girls and Native Sons: Female Images in Selected Works by Richard Wright." Trotman 59–77.

Webb, Constance. *Richard Wright: A Biography*. New York: Putnam, 1968.

White, Deborah Gray. *Ar'n't I a Woman: Female Slaves in the Plantation South*. New York: Norton, 1985.

Wideman, John Edgar. Introduction. *The Souls of Black Folk*. By W. E. B. Du Bois. New York: Vintage–Library of America, 1990. xi–xvi.

———. Preface. *Breaking Ice: An Anthology of Contemporary African-American Fiction*. Ed. Terry McMillan. New York: Penguin, 1990. v–x.

Widmer, Kingsley. "Black Existentialism: Richard Wright." Macksey and Moorer 173–81.

Williams, John A. *The Most Native of Sons: A Biography of Richard Wright*. Garden City: Doubleday, 1970.

———. "The Use of Communications Media in Four Novels by Richard Wright." *Callaloo* 9 (1986): 529–37.

Williams, Raymond. "Work." *Keywords: A Vocabulary of Culture and Society*. New York: Oxford UP, 1983. 334–47.

Williams, Sherley Anne. "Papa Dick and Sister-Woman: Reflections on Women in the Fiction of Richard Wright." Fleischmann 394–415.

Wolfram, Walt. "Beyond Black English: Implications of the Ann Arbor Decision for Other Non-mainstream Varieties." *Reactions to Ann Arbor: Vernacular Black English and Education*. Ed. Marcia Farr Whiteman. Arlington: Center for Applied Linguistics, 1980. 10–23.

Wright, Ellen, and Michel Fabre, eds. *Richard Wright Reader*. New York: Harper, 1978.

Wright, Richard. "Almos' a Man." *Harper's Bazaar* Jan. 1940: 40+.

———. *American Hunger*. New York: Harper, 1977.

———. *Black Boy: A Record of Childhood and Youth*. New York: Harper, 1945.

———. "Blueprint for Negro Writing." *New Challenge* 2 (1937): 53–65. Rpt. in Wright and Fabre 36–49.

———. "The Ethics of Living Jim Crow: An Autobiographical Sketch." *American Stuff*. Federal Writers' Project anthology. New York: Viking, 1937.

———. "How Bigger Was Born." Wright, *Native Son* [1966]. vii–xxxiv.

———. Introduction. Drake and Cayton xvii–xxxiv.

———. "I Tried to Be a Communist." *Atlantic Monthly* Aug. 1944: 61–70; Sept. 1944: 48–56. Rpt. in Crossman 115–62.

———. *Native Son*. New York: Harper, 1940. New York: HarperPerennial, 1966.

———. *Native Son*. 1991 [Restored]. Ed. Arnold Rampersad. New York: Library of America, 1992.

———. "Reply to David L. Cohn." Wright and Fabre 62–67. Rpt. of "I Bite the Hand That Feeds Me." *Atlantic Monthly* June 1940.

———. *Twelve Million Black Voices*. New York: Thunder's Mouth, 1988.

———. *Uncle Tom's Children*. 1938. New York: Perennial-Harper, 1965.

INDEX

Aaron, Daniel, 7
Algren, Nelson, 5, 8
Appiah, K. A., 6
Aswell, Edward, 52, 118
Awkward, Michael, 55

Baker, Houston A., Jr., 5, 6, 7, 121
Bakish, David, 4
Baldwin, James, 3, 5, 34, 44, 45
Bates, Karen Grisby, 53
Bell, Bernard W., 7
Benson, Joseph, 4
Bentham, Jeremy, 95
Bérubé, Michael, 15
Blassingame, John, 6
Bloom, Harold, 3, 5, 45, 90
Bogus, SDiane A., 14
Bone, Robert, 4, 5, 7, 104
Bontemps, Arna, 5
Boyd, Melba Joyce, 13
Bozziock, Joseph, 5
Bradley, David, 120
Brasmer, William, 18
Brignano, Russell, 4
Brown, Cecil, 5
Bühler, Karl, 33
Bumpurs, Eleanor, 124, 126
Butler, Robert J., 4, 13

Campbell, Ouida, 18
Cappetti, Carla, 8
Carby, Hazel, 46
Carter, Dan T., 6
Cassuto, Leonard, 14
Cather, Willa, 22
Cayton, Horace, 3, 6, 11
Charnak, Maurice, 5
Christian, Barbara, 59
Ciner, Elizabeth, 5
Cleaver, Eldridge, 5, 56, 60–62
Cobbs, Price, 6
Cohn, David, 49–50
Cooke, Michael G., 7
Cowley, Malcolm, 5
Crevecoeur, J. Hector St. John, 22, 23
Crew, Spencer R., 6
Crossman, Richard, 7
Cruse, Harold, 3, 6
Cunard, Nancy, 43

Darwin, Charles, 94
Davis, Benjamin, 105
Davis, Benjamin, Jr., 113, 118
Davis, Charles T., 4
Davis, Jane, 30
Davis, Randall C., 74

Deleuze, Gilles, 82
Dickens, Charles, 68
Dixon, Melvin, 7
Doane, Mary Ann, 77
Dollard, John, 6
Dostoevsky, Fyodor, 7, 22, 23
Douglas, Robert L., 5
Douglass, Frederick, 22
Drake, St. Clair, 3, 6, 11
Dreiser, Theodore, 7
Du Bois, W. E. B., 6, 13, 28, 44, 48, 51, 52
Duke, Bill, 53
Duke, David, 39

Ellis, Trey, 117, 119
Ellison, Ralph, 3, 23, 34, 44, 45, 117, 121
Emmanuel, James, 5

Fabian, Johannes, 73
Fabre, Michel, 3, 4, 8, 96, 100
Fanon, Frantz, 56, 58, 62, 63, 66
Farrell, James T., 8
Felgar, Cynthia, 74
Felgar, Robert, 4, 14
Fishburn, Katherine, 4
Fisher, Dorothy Canfield, 5, 52, 117, 118
Flower, Linda, 21
Foley, Barbara, 6
Foner, Philip S., 6
Ford, Nick Aaron, 5
Foucault, Michel, 14, 95–96, 97, 101
France, Alan, 30
Franklin, John Hope, 3, 6
Freire, Paulo, 83
Freud, Sigmund, 90, 91–92, 94

Gallagher, Kathleen, 121
Gates, Henry Louis, Jr., 6, 7, 28, 31, 51, 53
Gayle, Addison, Jr., 4, 7
Genovese, Eugene, 6
Gibson, Donald, 5, 7, 22, 23, 93
Gilbert, James, 7
Gillespie, Dizzy, 20
Giovanni, Nikki, 58
Giroux, Henry, 83
Gogol, Nikolai, 22
Gombrich, E. H., 51
Green, Paul, 16, 18–19, 20, 44
Grier, William, 6
Griffin, Farah Jasmine, 14
Griffith, Michael, 126
Grossman, James, 6
Guattari, Felix, 82
Guthrie, Ken, 74

Hakutani, Yoshinobu, 5, 7

Hall, James C., 14
Hansen, Harry, 22
Harris, Trudier, 30, 71, 121
Hawkins, Yusef, 60, 126
Hill, Herbert, 5
Holcomb, Jeri, 74
Horton, Willie, 13, 39, 71
Howe, Irving, 5, 117
Huggins, Nathan Irvin, 69
Hughes, Langston, 23, 42, 45, 46
Hurst, Fannie, 43
Hurston, Zora Neale, 23, 42, 45, 46

Ibsen, Henrik, 22
Ionesco, Eugene, 22

Jack, Peter Monro, 118
Jakobson, Roman, 33
James, Henry, 22
Johnson, Barbara E., 6, 33, 105
Joiner, Charles, 31
Joyce, Joyce Ann, 3, 4, 6, 31, 55

Kelley, Robin D. G., 7
Kent, George, 3, 5
King, Martin Luther, Jr., 11
Kinnamon, Keneth, 3, 4, 5, 6, 17–18, 48,
    52, 118
Kostelanetz, Richard, 5
Kurokawa, Kisho, 81–82

Lampert, Anja, 30, 31
Lee, Robert A., 93
Lee, Spike, 15, 61, 71, 122–25, 126
Levine, Lawrence, 6
Locke, Alain, 22
Lynch, Michael F., 7
Lyotard, Jean-François, 74

Macksey, Richard, 5
Magistrale, Tony, 7
Major, Clarence, 32
Mancino, Patrizia, 34
Margolies, Edward, 4, 102
Mason, Mrs. Rufus Osgood, 43
McCall, Dan, 4, 5
McCluskey, John, 31
McCormick, Kathleen, 21
Meier, August, 6
Miller, Eugene E., 4
Miller, James A., 77, 118, 121, 123
Moorer, Frank E., 5
Mootry, Maria, 5, 30
Moynihan, Daniel Patrick, 39
Murphy, James F., 7
Murray, Albert, 82

Naison, Mark, 6
Naylor, Gloria, 23
Nelles, Simon, 32
Newlin, Paul, 5, 89, 93
Nixon, Robert, 47, 116, 118

Petry, Ann, 80
Podhoretz, Norman, 60–61
Poovey, Mary, 68
Pudaloff, Ross, 6

Quinn, Laura L., 13

Record, Wilson, 7
Redding, J. Saunders, 5
Reed, Kenneth T., 7
Reilly, John, 4, 5, 48, 51, 105, 118
Rideout, Walter B., 7
Riggs, Marlon, 56
Robinson, Cedric, 6
Rooney, Ellen, 67, 68
Rosenblatt, Louise M., 68, 69
Rubin, Stephen J., 7
Rudwick, Elliott, 6

Sartre, Jean-Paul, 56, 57, 64, 66
Satz, Martha, 13
Schmidt, Klaus, 13
Schuhmacher, Annette, 31
Scott, Nathan A., 7
Shakespeare, William, 69
Shapiro, Herbert, 7
Siegal, Paul, 5
Silone, Ignazio, 22
Silverman, Kaja, 77
Skerrett, Joseph T., Jr., 5
Smallwood, Yvonne, 124, 126
Smith, Lillian, 62
Smith, Valerie, 7, 45
Smith, Virginia Whatley, 14
Snead, James, 100
Snipes, Wesley, 71
Soitos, Stephen, 5
Standley, Fred, 5
Steinbeck, John, 22
Stepto, Robert, 7, 52, 113, 121
Stewart, Michael, 124, 126
Stimpson, Catharine, 55, 60
Storhoff, Gary, 15

Tanner, Laura E., 6, 45
Tate, Beverly Daniel, 84
Theroux, Paul, 22
Thoreau, Henry David, 22
Till, Emmett, 60
Tremaine, Louis, 122

Trotman, James C., 3
Tyson, Mike, 112, 113

Van Vechten, Carl, 43

Walker, Alice, 23
Walker, Margaret, 3, 4
Wallace, Michelle, 61
Waller, Gary, 21
Ward, Jerry W., Jr., 13
Warren, Nagueyalti, 6, 30
Webb, Constance, 4
Werner, Craig, 4

White, Deborah Gray, 62
White, Garrett H., 13
Whitman, Walt, 22
Wideman, John Edgar, 34, 48
Widmer, Kingsley, 5, 8
Williams, John A., 4, 22, 119
Williams, Lisa M., 74
Williams, Raymond, 99
Williams, Sherley Anne, 30
Wolfram, Walt, 31

Zola, Emile, 22, 23

Modern Language Association of America
Approaches to Teaching World Literature
Joseph Gibaldi, series editor

Achebe's Things Fall Apart. Ed. Bernth Lindfors. 1991.

Arthurian Tradition. Ed. Maureen Fries and Jeanie Watson. 1992.

Atwood's The Handmaid's Tale *and Other Works.* Ed. Sharon R. Wilson, Thomas B. Friedman, and Shannon Hengen. 1996.

Austen's Pride and Prejudice. Ed. Marcia McClintock Folsom. 1993.

Beckett's Waiting for Godot. Ed. June Schlueter and Enoch Brater. 1991.

Beowulf. Ed. Jess B. Bessinger, Jr., and Robert F. Yeager. 1984.

Blake's Songs of Innocence and of Experience. Ed. Robert F. Gleckner and Mark L. Greenberg. 1989.

Brontë's Jane Eyre. Ed. Diane Long Hoeveler and Beth Lau. 1993.

Byron's Poetry. Ed. Frederick W. Shilstone. 1991.

Camus's The Plague. Ed. Steven G. Kellman. 1985.

Cather's My Ántonia. Ed. Susan J. Rosowski. 1989.

Cervantes' Don Quixote. Ed. Richard Bjornson. 1984.

Chaucer's Canterbury Tales. Ed. Joseph Gibaldi. 1980.

Chopin's The Awakening. Ed. Bernard Koloski. 1988.

Coleridge's Poetry and Prose. Ed. Richard E. Matlak. 1991.

Dante's Divine Comedy. Ed. Carole Slade. 1982.

Dickens' David Copperfield. Ed. Richard J. Dunn. 1984.

Dickinson's Poetry. Ed. Robin Riley Fast and Christine Mack Gordon. 1989.

Eliot's Middlemarch. Ed. Kathleen Blake. 1990.

Eliot's Poetry and Plays. Ed. Jewel Spears Brooker. 1988.

Ellison's Invisible Man. Ed. Susan Resneck Parr and Pancho Savery. 1989.

Faulkner's The Sound and the Fury. Ed. Stephen Hahn and Arthur F. Kinney. 1996.

Flaubert's Madame Bovary. Ed. Laurence M. Porter and Eugene F. Gray. 1995.

García Márquez's One Hundred Years of Solitude. Ed. María Elena de Valdés and Mario J. Valdés. 1990.

Goethe's Faust. Ed. Douglas J. McMillan. 1987.

Hebrew Bible as Literature in Translation. Ed. Barry N. Olshen and Yael S. Feldman. 1989.

Homer's Iliad *and* Odyssey. Ed. Kostas Myrsiades. 1987.

Ibsen's A Doll House. Ed. Yvonne Shafer. 1985.

Works of Samuel Johnson. Ed. David R. Anderson and Gwin J. Kolb. 1993.

Joyce's Ulysses. Ed. Kathleen McCormick and Erwin R. Steinberg. 1993.

Kafka's Short Fiction. Ed. Richard T. Gray. 1995.

Keats's Poetry. Ed. Walter H. Evert and Jack W. Rhodes. 1991.

Kingston's The Woman Warrior. Ed. Shirley Geok-lin Lim. 1991.

Lessing's The Golden Notebook. Ed. Carey Kaplan and Ellen Cronan Rose. 1989.

Mann's Death in Venice *and Other Short Fiction.* Ed. Jeffrey B. Berlin. 1992.

Medieval English Drama. Ed. Richard K. Emmerson. 1990.

Melville's Moby-Dick. Ed. Martin Bickman. 1985.

Metaphysical Poets. Ed. Sidney Gottlieb. 1990.

Miller's Death of a Salesman. Ed. Matthew C. Roudané. 1995.

Milton's Paradise Lost. Ed. Galbraith M. Crump. 1986.

Molière's Tartuffe *and Other Plays.* Ed. James F. Gaines and Michael S. Koppisch. 1995.

Momaday's The Way to Rainy Mountain. Ed. Kenneth M. Roemer. 1988.

Montaigne's Essays. Ed. Patrick Henry. 1994.

Murasaki Shikibu's The Tale of Genji. Ed. Edward Kamens. 1993.

Pope's Poetry. Ed. Wallace Jackson and R. Paul Yoder. 1993.

Shakespeare's King Lear. Ed. Robert H. Ray. 1986.

Shakespeare's The Tempest *and Other Late Romances.* Ed. Maurice Hunt. 1992.

Shelley's Frankenstein. Ed. Stephen C. Behrendt. 1990.

Shelley's Poetry. Ed. Spencer Hall. 1990.

Sir Gawain and the Green Knight. Ed. Miriam Youngerman Miller and Jane Chance. 1986.

Spenser's Faerie Queene. Ed. David Lee Miller and Alexander Dunlop. 1994.

Sterne's Tristram Shandy. Ed. Melvyn New. 1989.

Swift's Gulliver's Travels. Ed. Edward J. Rielly. 1988.

Thoreau's Walden *and Other Works.* Ed. Richard J. Schneider. 1996.

Voltaire's Candide. Ed. Renée Waldinger. 1987.

Whitman's Leaves of Grass. Ed. Donald D. Kummings. 1990.

Wordsworth's Poetry. Ed. Spencer Hall, with Jonathan Ramsey. 1986.

Wright's Native Son. Ed. James A. Miller. 1997.